The Outdoor Grandparent

From Backyard to Wilderness

Ruby Robinson

D1521497

Introduction

The best inheritance a person can leave to his grand-children is not money, but a legacy of memories and life lessons. Unknown

I had no idea of the nature of the adventure I was about to enter until that very special day when I held my first grandchild.

When I use the word 'adventure', I'm not only referring to the many, fun-filled trips I had with them (I have three now). I'm also referring to the wonderful and exciting opportunity I have as a grand-parent to make a lasting impact on their lives, leave a positive mark on the younger generation, be part of their upbringing and helping to shape their personalities. I've been granted the opportunity to pass on knowledge and play an integral part in my grandkids' growth and development. But also, I've been blessed to have my life shaped by their curiosity and perspective on a world in which I became so blasé in my more mature age. It's a chance to relive the joys of childhood through the eyes of your grandchildren while imparting wisdom and creating lasting memories.

For adventurous grandparents, there's hardly any more exciting and effective backdrop for bonding and exploration than the great outdoors. Imagine the excitement on your grandchild's face as you teach them how to pitch a tent, start a campfire or identify different bird calls.

These moments of connection and discovery are priceless.

The Benefits of Spending Time in the Great Outdoors

It's no secret that spending time in the great outdoors is beneficial for kids of all ages, but do you know exactly how beneficial it is?

While there are many more benefits to enjoy, some of the more celebrated benefits are:

- **Learning life skills** like self-regulation of behavior and emotions, taking responsibility for their decisions and regulating their impulses.

- **The potential for improved eyesight**. Did you know that **near-sightedness** is an increasing problem among young children? Research in the field of optometry found that children who spend more time in nature are less likely to develop this vision impairment (9 Reasons Why Kids Should Spend Time in Nature, 2023).

- **Improved emotional and mental well-being**. Spending time in green spaces has gained traction over recent years, as it has many benefits for emotional and mental well-being. This is no different for children. Time in nature **improves their mood, boosts their self-esteem and supports over-**

all emotional well-being in even the youngest grandchild.

* **Becoming healthier.** *Childhood obesity* has become more prolific and is a major concern. Spending time in the great outdoors is an effective way to encourage more activity and reduce the focus on any weight concerns, allowing activity to lead to a natural balance.

* **Stimulating their imagination**. Nature is a place where **imagination can go wild.** Depending on your circumstances and environment, you may find yourself needing a greater level of creativity. Hence, it's the perfect place to encourage creative play, setting the foundation for creative thinking as they grow older.

* **Recharging the brain**. The natural environment **encourages critical thinking, problem-solving and resilience, and is a welcomed relief from mental fatigue, often associated with spending many hours in school.** Taking breaks from school to spend time in nature is a wonderful way to establish balance that will improve their academic performance.

* Instilling a **love for nature** in them from an early age onwards, turning the next generation into caring stalwarts of the planet.

The list goes on and serves as confirmation that the more time you spend with your grandkids in nature, the better it is for them and you. By introducing them to the wonderful and magical outdoors, you're creating cherished memories and contributing to their overall well-being. But being outside and spending time in the outdoors is also good for you. It uplifts the mood, gives you energy and strength, and reduces feelings of isolation.

However, many grandparents feel uncertain about how to plan age-appropriate outdoor activities or adapt adventures for different ability levels.

- Do you worry about safety concerns or struggle to keep up with your energetic grandchildren?

- Are you keen to step outside with your grandchildren but don't know what they're old enough to enjoy?

- Do you sometimes wonder if you'll manage to keep them safe when you're outdoors?

What to Expect From This Book

The Outdoor Grandparent—From Backyard to Wilderness is your comprehensive guide to creating unforgettable outdoor experiences with your grandchildren, no matter their age or ability level. It offers a wealth of ideas for engaging activities, from nature scavenger hunts for toddlers to adrenaline-pumping adventures for teens.

But this book is more than just a collection of activity ideas.

It's a roadmap for strengthening family bonds and passing down a love of nature to future generations. You'll learn how to talk effectively with your grandchildren, foster their curiosity and independence, and create a safe and supportive environment for exploration.

Whether you're a seasoned outdoors person or a novice, this book will equip you with the knowledge and confidence to set off on exciting adventures with your grandchildren.

You'll discover tips and tricks for making the most of your time together, such as how to turn a simple hike into a fun-filled learning experience or how to adapt popular outdoor games for different age groups.

As a grandparent, you have a unique opportunity to shape your grandchildren's lives and create lasting memories. By embracing the role of an adventurous grandparent, you'll deepen your bond with your grandchildren and help them develop valuable life skills such as resilience, problem-solving and appreciation for the natural world.

Are you ready to take on this adventure? Let's take the first step of this exciting quest together!

Contents

Chapter 1

Preparing for Outdoor Adventures With Your Grandchildren

"Nobody can do for little children what grandparents do. Grandparents sort of sprinkle stardust over the lives of little children." – Alex Haley

"I was stuck on the ground! I promise you; I couldn't move a thing! And there he went off running. I shouted, 'Stop! Danny, come to Nana', but what did he know? I was amazed at how fast those short legs could go. If it wasn't for Gary, I don't know how the day would've ended."

"Who's Gary?" we all wanted to know.

"Oh, Gary. He sleeps on one of the benches in the park. Nice fellow. He saw the entire spectacle: me doing somersaults; the great fall; the runaway; and managed to catch Danny. Making one heck of a racket of course! But he brought him back and helped me up," Gina continued her story of complete humiliation.

Our group of friends, all in our senior years, was hiking one of the least challenging trails just outside the city. It was a magnificent morning, perfect for hiking. It was early, but clear skies were all around us, making it evident that today would be a marvelous day to be outside. As we progressed on the winding pathway between tall-growing trees with scattered glimpses of the valley below, there were moments of complete silence as we took in everything around us with a deep-rooted sense of gratitude. Then, there were also moments of chatter, mostly laughter, especially once we start sharing the moments when our physical abilities had left us lacking. Let's just say, some of those moments were not our proudest.

"But Gina," Sarah (the conservative one in the group) wanted to know, "What made you think you can still do somersaults and get away with it?"

"Oh well, because I was the Queen of Somersaults! It might have been 50 years ago, but I was the Queen back then!" Gina proudly defended her former title.

The point of the story is that it's easy to overestimate your abilities if you're still feeling fit and are young at heart, but doing so, and getting yourself in a pickle when you're the one looking after your grandkids, can place them at risk and may limit your freedom to take them places. It only takes one mistake, a tiny slip-up, to shatter the trust your kids have in you to take care of their babies.

The best way to be sure you're up to whatever outdoor adventure you're planning is to do a proper fitness assessment.

Assessing Your Fitness Level

Your fitness level will largely determine your capabilities as an active grandparent and being active will also lead to longevity and lasting vitality (at least, that's what the active grandparent hypothesis states). But more on that later. For now, let's explore how you can determine your fitness level and whether you're capable of keeping up with your grandkids.

Why am I hammering on so much about fitness and knowing what you're physically capable of doing as a grandparent? Simply because grandparenting is, to a large extent, a sport in its own right.

From the moment your first grandchild arrives, you'll most likely find yourself picking them up and using muscles you may not have used in a long time. You'll be up and down, bending over forward and rocking the little one to sleep. You'll be on your hands and knees, crawling on the floor, chasing them in the garden and getting up from the floor (that can be the worst). But if you're not fit and try to do all that, you might find yourself sore and sorry when it is too late.

For the most part, you'll know whether you're up for it or not, but the following exercises will also serve as an excellent guide to give you either the confidence that you're perhaps better equipped to do it, or it will tell you where you need to shape up, even if just slightly.

Fitness Test Exercises

Balance, mobility, stamina and grip strength are the four pillars on which your success as an active grandparent rests.

- **Balance** refers to how stable you are and whether you're at risk of tripping or falling over. The best way to test this is to test your leg strength in each leg separately. The exercise that portrays this the clearest is called The Stork and is pretty much what the name implies.

  - Stand barefoot close to a chair or a door offering support if needed

  - Keep your eyes open at all times as it is much harder to maintain your balance with eyes closed

  - Now, lift one leg and maintain your balance on the other

  - Time how long you can hold your pose

  - Ideally, you want to be able to hold your position for at least 45 seconds. Anything better is a bonus. But if you didn't make it to 30 seconds, I'd suggest doing some Pilates exercises to improve your ability. Improving your balance will benefit your life in many more ways than only being an amazing, active grandparent.

- **Mobility.** Joint issues usually hamper mobility and while it can be painful, it can also limit one's ability to enjoy one's grandkids.

  - Find a sturdy chair with a straight back that won't tip over

  - Set your timer and see how many times you can stand up and sit down without using your hands in 30 seconds

○ Ideally, you want to do so 13 to 14 times

- **Stamina.** To test for stamina, you can either run or walk a mile. It truly depends on what you're comfortable doing. Ideally, you should be able to walk a mile within 16 to 17 minutes and if you're more confident and opt for running, then you should aim for 12 to 13 minutes.

- **Grip strength.** This is the last but not least exercise you should test as you'll be holding the most precious cargo — your grandchild. This is another toughie and again, I urge you to take care not to injure yourself. If at first you can't manage it, exercise the necessary muscles to improve rather than force your body to do something it just can't do.

  ○ Pull yourself up on a pull-up bar or even a doorway and see how long you can maintain your grip. Ideally, you want to hold on for 10 seconds.

The Active Grandparent Hypothesis

The specific theory stems from research done by the National Academy of Sciences, determining that during the days when survival depended on hunting and gathering food, elders in the tribe (the few who lived past child-bearing age) could contribute to the well-being of the tribe by looking after the children. Furthermore, it is believed that this increased level of activity is what kept them alive longer (Reynolds, 2022).

Today, we know that increased activity contributes to health and well-being. This lesson is further confirmed when we explore life in the

Blue Zones of the world. These are the five zones in the world where people tend to get very old and easily reach 100 years of age.

One of the common factors we notice in all these five areas is to be active with a purpose. This is also called N.E.A.T. or Non-Exercise Activity Thermogenesis (Almekinder, 2020). While many of the older residents of these areas turn to gardening or visiting their friends on foot to stay active, I think that there can hardly be any activity more rewarding than looking after your grandkids. So, while being fit can make it easier to be the grandparent you want to be, it'll also help you to stay around for your grandkids a little longer. That's what I call a win-win situation!

Once an acceptable level of fitness has been established, it's time to start preparing for an outdoor adventure.

Essential Gear and Equipment for Outdoor Excursions

The essential equipment you'll need to have on hand to have a fun time outdoors with your grandkids will largely depend on what kind of activity you're planning and the age of your grandkids. For instance, your packing list will differ slightly whether you're planning to go camping compared to when you're looking forward to a day of hiking. Similarly, it'll also vary between what you pack for toddlers and preteens. So, I'm sharing a general list of basic gear and equipment that'll come in handy during various kinds of adventures. These are in no order of importance and are merely a list of things I find helpful to have on hand.

1. **Water bottles and food containers**. Children get hungry and thirsty at the most inconvenient times and when they do, there's hardly any time to spare before you may have a complete, emotional meltdown on your hands. So, it's best to come prepared so you can offer whatever they need, when they need it. Opt for items that are lightweight, long-lasting and can take the bumps and tumbles along the way.

2. **Backpack child carrier**. This is especially helpful to have if you're planning to cover long walks with a small child. Sure, they'll want to walk themselves at times, but their legs won't be up to it all the time. A carrier can help include small kids in the adventure while also being a hands-free option for you. Choose a carrier that is lightweight and yet sturdy, offers a comfortable fit and has a shade or outer cover to protect your grandchild against some of the natural elements.

3. **Comfortable shoes for water and hiking.** Wearing the wrong shoes will be uncomfortable, cause blisters and can quickly suck all the fun out of an adventure. Choose shoes for them that are the right fit, offer proper protection and are lightweight. Other features to look out for are quick-drying, being machine-washable and being able to take on or off easily while still offering a secure fit. A good idea if you have the space, is to have lightweight footwear for crossing small streams and the like. There's nothing worse than hiking in wet shoes.

4. **Sun protection.** While proper sunscreen is a must to protect their skin and avoid the discomfort of sunburn, you should also ensure they wear hats and see if you can find clothes with

a high enough UPF rating.

5. **Clothing.** This should be light and layered, offer sufficient warmth during colder conditions, but also allow you to take off the layers as the day warms up. Depending on the weather forecast, you may also want to consider rain gear to keep them dry. Rain boots can be a wonderful addition as they keep their feet dry, offer comfort during walking and can help encourage their spirit of exploration to surface. A good pair of socks is another must! Good socks will keep their feet dry, allow for breathing and offer comfort. Always have a spare pair on hand.

6. **Backpack for kids.** Older kids especially may like to carry their own food or have a bag where they can keep the treasures found along the way. Great backpacks to consider are lightweight, easy to put on or take off and, of course, waterproof.

7. **Headlamps.** There are so many different types of headlamps available these days, but, essentially, you want something 'hands-free' that will offer light when you're overnighting in the outdoors or are planning on exploring caves or dark spaces. Pack spare batteries to be sure that your hands-free solutions can keep on shining regardless for as long as you need them.

8. **Compass.** Today, there are so many smart gadgets available to help find your way that a compass may seem outdated. However, compasses can make for an amazing conversation starter and will usually intrigue younger generations. It may

also present an opportunity to impart some of your wisdom to your grandkids. Make sure you know how to use a compass yourself so you can demonstrate its use firsthand. A compass also makes a wonderful gift to the older child who shows a real interest in nature, hiking and exploring the outdoors.

9. **Binoculars.** A great pair of binoculars opens an entirely different world. It enables your grandchildren to see birds flying high in the sky, finding the trail, identifying animals in the distance or simply staring off in the distance to see what is happening on the horizon. Binoculars also make for an exciting conversation about how to take care of your camping equipment.

10. **Bug spray.** Creepy crawlies are at home in nature and we're stepping into their territory. While it can be a lot of fun to be close to them, it's more often than not the case that we don't want them on us. Bites can be nasty and turn a happy kid into a very miserable one. So, always pack sufficient bug spray that is safe not only for your grandchild, but also for the environment.

11. **Sleeping bags.** Campfire stories are best followed up by slipping into a sleeping bag and staring at the stars until sleep gets the better of you. The quality of your sleeping bag will determine whether you wake up well-rested or suffer through a night of cold discomfort and it's no different for your grandkids. Shop around to find the best quality at the most affordable price. Feather and/or down bags are very warm and light but provide little to no warmth when wet, so

also think about synthetic bag options which are often less expensive.

12. **Tents.** These should be light to carry, waterproof and large enough to fit your entire party. Here again, looking for quality would be a key factor in making sure your adventure with your grandkids is enjoyable. Remember, pitching a tent often happens at the end of the day when everyone is often tired or even exhausted. Don't punish yourself with a tent demanding an engineering degree to pitch. Another tip is to make sure you have pitched the tent at home so you're familiar with the task.

13. **Chairs.** While camping chairs aren't a necessity, they sure are nice to have. However, packing them will be decided by the type of adventure you're on, how much hiking is involved and the age of your grandkids.

So, there you have it! That's my list of my 13 essentials. While you may be able to make do without them, having them surely makes life outdoors a lot easier. But there is one more essential I haven't yet mentioned and that brings me to the issue of First Aid.

Safety First !

First Aid Kits and Skills

The 14th essential on my list is a first aid kit. There's so much to say about safety and first aid and, unfortunately, we won't be able to cover it all here but we will cover some of the essentials and recommend you get some approved training.

There is, without a doubt, a certain sense of comfort and confidence rooted in knowing that you're prepared for any event while enjoying outdoor adventures with your grandkids. This level of preparedness rests on two pillars: having the necessary first aid essentials in your kit; and knowing how to use them when a medical emergency arises. The preferred choice is that you'll never need to use your first aid kit or have to fall back on your first aid skills, but it is one of those life scenarios that you'd rather be prepared for and not need, rather than needing them and not having them.

But first, let me share a story about Gene and Carla, a wonderful couple we became friends with during some of our outdoor adventures.

"Gene thought he was dying," the somewhat dramatic Carla shared as the adults settled in around the campfire after our grandkids had all been tucked in for the night.

We were on night two of a three-day camping adventure and Gene and Carla were camping at the same river site we'd chosen to spend time with our grandkids.

Carla continued, "We were out all day, climbing over rocks and jumping small streams. It was just the most amazing setting. Gene, you must tell them all about it when I'm done."

Gene simply sunk deeper into his camping chair knowing that he was again about to be humiliated, but he also knew there was no stopping his wife once she was on a roll.

Carla carried on regardless and even started to pick up the pace. "The kids got hungry and thirsty and so did we. There was plenty to eat, but not the healthiest kind of snacks, I must say. However, it didn't matter as the kids were busy and happy. We were all burning lots of calories on the walk and just about five fingers before the sun hit the horizon, we arrived at our camping spot. The kids helped Gene pitch the tent and I was starting with supper when I heard this awful groan coming from Gene as he collapsed. I got such a fright. I turned around and saw he looked awfully pale and sweaty. I thought, 'Oh, golly, Gene is having a heart attack right here under the trees. What will I do?' Gene could hardly speak. He was holding his chest and I could see he was in a lot of pain. The kids started crying and I thought I was going to lose my marbles! Then, low and behold, my cellphone rang. Can you believe it? Reception out there! It was Tina, the twins' mom who wanted to know if we were okay. I was hysterical and told her everything. Tina thankfully arranged for an ER chopper from her side. It was the whole palaver! The chopper found us between the trees, landed and two guys came running with a stretcher and some equipment. By then I had managed to get the kids into the tent while I sat with Gene, who by now had started to look somewhat better. You know, though, you don't recover from a heart attack just like that. And the reason? It wasn't a heart attack!." Carla abruptly stopped her story and looked over at Gene.

"Well, what was it?" I wanted to know.

"Gas," Gene said with a voice of resignation.

"All just gas from his acid reflux and all the bad eating during the day," Carla ended with a smile (and a slight hint of blame in her voice), "Just gas!"

So, coming back from that story to our topic, it can be so easy to get consumed by thinking only about your grandkids, keeping them safe and what they may need while you're out and about, that you completely forget to take care of your own needs. For instance, if you suffer from acid reflux, as Gene did, be sure to pack those antacids to keep bad digestion from spoiling your adventures.

Taking care of yourself is also a preventative measure you need to consider in your first aid planning.

That now brings us to what you should have in your first aid kit. The following list will provide you with a great foundation of what is needed, but also, you should always consider your personal needs and any medical conditions your grandchildren may have. For instance, if you know one of your grandkids is allergic to bees, be sure to have that *EpiPen* packed.

What to Pack in a Basic First Aid Kit

- Antiseptic wipes

- Antibacterial ointment

- Compound tincture of benzoin

- Assorted adhesive bandages

- Triangle bandages

- Butterfly bandages / adhesive wound-closure strips

- Gauze pads

- Scissors

- Surgical gloves

- Nonstick sterile pads

- Medical adhesive tape

- Blister treatment

- Ibuprofen or any other pain-relief medication like aspirin or paracetamol

- Insect sting or anti-itch treatment

- Antihistamine to treat allergic reactions

- Tweezers

- Tick removal tool

- Safety pins

- Pencil

- Small notepad

- First-aid manual or information cards

- Half roll mat

Additional Aids to Add

While the basics will already get you a long way, more aids can be helpful to have in certain crises. These things are:

- Elastic wrap

- Liquid bandages

- Finger splints

- SAM splints

- Hydrogel pads

- Sunburn relief gel or spray

- Glucose syrup

- Antacid tablets

- Diarrhea medication

- Throat lozenges

- Eye drops

- Rehydration salts

- Hand sanitizer

First Aid Kit Tools

The following tools will also be handy:

- Knife or multi-tool

- Medical waste bag

- Syringe

- CPR mask

- Heat-reflecting blanket

- Thermometer

- Cotton-tipped swabs

- Biodegradable soap

- Waterproof container to hold supplies

- Safety razor blade

- Paramedic shears

While these things are all handy to have, they'll mean nothing if you don't have the skills to use them effectively. So, we also need to look at the first aid skills you need to be comfortable with to be sure you can take care of yourself and your grandkids while in the great outdoors. Here are some of the basics to heighten your awareness about what might happen and, again, please get approved first aid training in these areas:

- **CPR.** Familiarize yourself with how to perform it and when it's necessary. The best option is to get proper CPR training so that an expert can show you exactly how it is done and you can practice on their dummies.

- **Sprained or twisted joints.** These injuries are quite common during hikes and walks, especially if you're on uneven territory. They can be extremely painful and will require immediate care. The RICE method is a trusted treatment option for these kinds of injuries:

  - **R**est: Take a break to stop any pain action worsening the injury.

  - **I**ce: If you don't have ice or an icepack, try to find anything cold to put on the injury for about 20 minutes three times daily.

  - **C**ompression: Place an elastic bandage around the injured joint. It should be tight but not so tight that it cuts off circulation.

  - **E**levation: Try to keep the injured area above heart level to reduce swelling to the area.

- **Splints for fractures.** A bad fall can easily cause a fracture. These, or even just a suspected fracture, must be kept stable to reduce pain and prevent further damage to the bone or surrounding tissue. The best way to do this is to tie makeshift splints securely around the fracture. Trekking poles are great for makeshift splints, but you can also use sturdy smooth, straight sticks or even wrap clothing around the fractured limb.

- **Blisters.** Uncomfortable socks or shoes are often the culprits for causing blisters. The best time to treat a blister is when it is just starting and, by applying a plaster early on, that will reduce friction and could save a lot of discomfort. Wash the area of the blister with soap and water and apply antibiotic ointment before covering it with a bandage. You may be tempted to pop a blister, but don't unless it is very big. You can buy blister donuts that work extremely well.

- **Stings.** These can put an immediate stop to your adventure as you'll have to attend to them first. If you can see the sting in the skin, use a sharp, hard object to remove it by scraping it out of the skin, being careful not to release any more venom into the skin. Wash the area with soap and water and apply ice or something cold. You can also use antihistamine ointment or topical creams to help with the itching and burning of the area.

- **Snake bites.** These can come with an immense shock as snake bites can be very dangerous and place you in a critical medical emergency. First, make sure it is a snake bite by checking the wound for two puncture marks. Keep the limb still and below heart level and call for help. Remove any tight-fitting clothes if there is any swelling and apply a pressure immobilization bandage for the arm or leg involved. Snake bites come with a few don'ts.

  - Don't cut the wound

  - Don't try to suck the poison out

  - Don't put a tourniquet around the affected area.

- **Allergic reactions.** Depending on the severity of the reaction, you may have to apply antihistamine ointment, give pills or use an EpiPen. Look out for a rash, swelling or trouble breathing to determine the necessary course of action.

- **Heat stroke.** Being outdoors can make you warm and if you're not properly hydrating, your body can easily go into a state of heat stroke. Symptoms are dizziness, nausea or excessive sweating. Immediately move the impacted person to a cooler area out of the sun. Give them fluids to drink and let them rest. If the situation doesn't improve, you'll need to get help.

There are a hundred more things you can do (or should know), but being equipped with these essential first-aid skills forms a necessary foundation to enable you to venture into the outdoors with your grandkids with at least enough confidence to enjoy the adventure.

Meal Planning and Snack Ideas for Energetic Outings

Eating in the great outdoors is as much about 'how' you're eating and preparing food as it is about 'what' you're eating. Sure, you need to include healthy, energy-boosting food to ensure everyone stays strong and energized, but it's also a lot of fun to have your grandkids help you prepare these meals and eat them together. Food preparation is a wonderful opportunity to pass on wisdom, have fun and create lasting memories.

Equip Yourself for Outdoor Cooking

What do you need to make a decent meal in the outdoors?

Typically, a camp kitchen will mostly consist of the list below, but a word of advice first—you don't have to buy it all for your first outdoor adventure! I suggest that you get some of the more basic pieces of equipment first and gradually expand your *kitchen* with what is right for you. Some of these items might be more suitable for backpacking and other heavier items more suitable for when you go with the car or 4Wheel Drive camping:

- Sharp knives

- Spatula

- Tongs

- Bowls

- Mixing spoons

- Bottle opener

- Cutting board

- Collapsible containers

- Dutch oven

- Dinnerware

- Kettle

- Mugs

- Pot scraper

- Cast iron cookware

- Camp stove

- Grill

Don't forget the dish soap and cloths or sponges to clean up afterward.

Now that we have your kitchen equipment set up and before you think about what to make, I've a few extra hacks to share:

- Try to prepare as much as you can in advance.

- Only bring food you know and they will love to eat.

- Choose options that require less space when packed.

- Bring a bit more than you think you'll need (all the activity and excitement may leave you and them hungry for more).

- Use a cooler to keep fresh foods as fresh as possible.

What Food to Pack

Some foods just make for great outdoor eating. While the recipes may differ, the following are often the staples, either as meals or snacks, when having outdoor adventures with the grandkids. Ideally, you'll want to provide them with nutrition and energy, finding the balance between food being a bit of a treat and being healthy.

- Hotdogs

- Muffins (savory)

- Fruit

- Tortillas

- Tacos

- Eggs (but do use a protective plastic container)

- Bacon

- Pasta

- Patties

- Pancakes

- Sandwiches

- S'mores (an absolute must!)

- Pies

- Beef jerky

- Granola bars

- Sausages

- Crackers

- Trail mix (cranberries, raisins, cashews, peanut butter chips, chocolate chips, marshmallows, honey-roasted peanuts)

- Plenty of things to drink (coffee, tea, juice, etc.)

Three-Day Meal Plan

How can you use these ingredients? Here is a three-day meal plan to ignite your imagination.

- Day one:

  - Breakfast—defrost savory muffins overnight and serve them with a hot beverage.

  - Lunch—grilled cheese sandwiches made on the open fire.

  - Dinner—hotdogs with s'mores for dessert.

- Day two:

  - Breakfast—pancakes and fresh fruit.

  - Lunch—grilled sausages and cut into pasta.

  - Dinner—tacos and filling of your choice

- Day three:

  - Breakfast—bacon and eggs.

  - Lunch—pies with fresh fruit.

  - Dinner—homemade burgers with grilled patties.

Now, that makes my mouth water!

The 'Outdoor Essentials Checklist' to Ensure You're Prepared

Are you good to go? Are you ready to have the first of many adventures making magnificent memories with your grandchildren?

Of course, you are, but I also know that it may still feel a little overwhelming. So, keep the following *Outdoor Essentials Checklist* handy to ensure that you don't miss anything when packing. You may not need everything on the following list (depending on where you're heading, how you're getting there and for how long), but adapt it to fit your needs and be sure you're well-equipped:

- Tent

- Pegs

- Peg bag

- Nylon rope

- Storm straps

- Hammer

- Groundsheet

- Tent repair kit

- Windbreaker

- Sleeping bags

- Camp chairs

- Camping tables

- Lanterns or flashlights

- Cable ties

- Pillows

- Firewood

- Duct tape

- Batteries

- Axe

- Knife or multi-tool

- Matches

- Hammock

- Camp shower

- Toilet paper

- Hand sanitizer

- Small spade

- Binoculars

- Trash bags

- Charcoal

- Kitchen utensils

- Tablecloth

- Storage containers

- Ropes

- Dishwashing stand

- Draining racks

- Dish towels

- Wash basin

- Bucket

- Cloths or rags

- Refuse bin

- Water container

- Clothes

- First aid kit

- Fire extinguisher

- Gas bottle

- Gas cooker top

- Clothesline

- Griddle

- Dutch oven

- Kettle

- Water jugs

What more can you add to the list?

Preparation is the key to success! The better you plan and prepare yourself for these adventures, the greater the fun you'll have with your grandkids.

Remember also to check for the weather, read up about your destination and plan for every kind of event that may occur so that you can ensure an exciting and memorable outing for all. Now that you're all set, it is time to explore various age-appropriate outings you can have with your grandkids, starting from as young as 0-3 years old.

Chapter 2

Baby & Toddler Adventures (Ages 0-3)

There are no words to describe the happiness of holding your baby's baby. Unknown

It was the cutest thing. Those lips looked just like a rosebud and the cheeks reminded me of two little pink balls of candy floss. Aah, I was instantly smitten as I laid my eyes on my first grandchild. I couldn't get myself to stop sniffing his head and holding his little fingers, and oh, that little bundle was so adorable.

Newborn babies are miracles. They're vulnerable and precious, and, at times, you may feel like you want to wrap these delicate little people in cotton wool to keep them safe. Holding your own baby is special and there's possibly nothing to beat that, but there is something different, so wonderful, about holding your grandchild. It's a proud moment, a moment when your heart will be bursting with love and, like your own child, you know you'll do anything to protect them.

So, it's understandable if you initially feel a little reluctant to take them outside. Understandably, young parents may have their reservations too, yet it's never too early to start your outdoor adventures.

Outdoor Baby Adventures Benefit Everyone

I do say 'everyone' because when it comes to taking your baby grand-kids on outdoor adventures, it's not only you and your grandchild standing to benefit, but mom and dad as well. Having a new addition to the family can be overwhelming and, for many couples, may be hard to make time for their partner or spouse and keep the relationship strong.

Becoming a first-time parent can be very time consuming and, at some point, the young mom or dad may feel like they just need a 'time out' to reset themselves, recharge their batteries and give their relationship the time it needs. These are important and healthy times for couples and their children will flourish when they can grow up in a home where there's a happy and healthy relationship between parents.

As a grandparent, you're standing to benefit from spending time with your grandkids and having the opportunity to forge a special bond early on. You'll spend more time outdoors, which is good for your mental and emotional wellbeing, and may also encourage you to be a bit more active.

But the one who'll enjoy the most benefit will be your grandbaby, for sure!

Time spent outdoors makes them happy, introduces them to a range of sensory experiences and helps to boost their immune systems. It's also an amazing way to foster their love for nature from a young age onward. You'll also find that some 'outside' time lets the baby sleep much better at night and sets the foundation to keep them immune to allergies. And did you also know that if you're living near the ocean, the salty sea air can also help to heal them?

Safety First!

As long as you take the necessary safety precautions, it's never too early to take your grandbaby outside. Safety, of course, comes first for then the fun lasts longer and the entire outdoor venture (even if only in the backyard) will also be a lot more fun.

- **Dress them for the weather** so that they're never too cold but also not too hot. That said, whatever they wear should still be comfortable and soft on their skin. Light cotton clothes are best for summer as they breathe and absorb sweat, leaving them dry and comfy the entire time. Fleece and wool are better options for winter to ensure they're cozy even when it is cold outside. Also, consider using layers that can be removed as the day warms up.

- **Sun protection is essential!** A baby's skin is extremely delicate and vulnerable to harsh UV rays. Remember that just because it may be overcast outside, it doesn't mean their skin won't burn. Even when it is snowed up, you still need to keep them safe from the rays reflecting off the snow. That said, some pediatricians advise that you keep a baby younger than six month entirely out of the sun and for older little ones, you should apply sunscreen up to SPF30. That doesn't mean that your very young grandchild can't go outside; just keep them out of direct sunlight at all times.

- **What about germs?** Young babies still have developing immune systems and while outdoor exposure is good for them, you still need to take the necessary precautions like washing hands and keeping them away from anything that can make them sick. When it comes to germ exposure, it's best to first dip in only a toe rather than take a deep dive straight away.

And, as you won't venture out far with the young ones and gear and safety kits won't be that much of a concern, be sure to have all they may need on hand, including all you need for that important nappy change.

Neighborhood Nature Walks — Awakening Wonder in Little Ones

Neighborhood walks are great because you don't have to take your grandbaby out of the stroller and can keep them warm and protected the entire time while you introduce them to the world. Have them in a comfortable position that allows them to see outside the stroller. It doesn't matter whether they're looking at the sky and clouds or treetops or are in a more upright position and can see ahead of them.

Even if they fall asleep, it's still okay. It just means that they're feeling safe in your company and that makes exploring the world where everything is new to them, much easier. While they're sleeping in the stroller, you'll still get some time in green spaces, mom and dad will get a break, and all that will happen while grandbaby is inhaling fresh air.

What does matter is that you let them have the lead. If your grandbaby is grumpy and not feeling well, they're not going to be interested in seeing anything new and the odds of them making negative connections with outdoor strolls will be much higher. For such times, focus only on being outdoors when everything lines up and the experience is an excellent one.

Once they're a little older, these adventures will become far more exciting for you both. By that age, they're likely associating your outdoor trips with positive feelings and may even want to walk a bit themselves. This is a good time to introduce them to new plants, flowers, seeds or little bugs.

Keep an eye open for all exciting and new objects to show them as you take a walk in nature. You can add extra fun with bubbles. The floating spheres reflect light in all colors and are mesmerizing to look at. The simple act of blowing bubbles will also be good for their fine motor skill development.

Having them wait for every burst of bubbles also sets the foundation for their emotional development to further take shape. In a world where almost everything is instantly available, we naturally tend to get addicted to instant gratification. Hence, it's good to establish from a young age onwards, an understanding that sometimes good things come to those who wait.

The Backyard Basecamp Approach

Introducing the Outdoors

"We had the most wonderful day planned. Everyone was up early, but Lacy doesn't allow anyone to sleep late. You know she's teething, already two teeth out. But they don't come easy for this one. There's a lot of crying and Sarah is already done."

My friend Priscilla is just lovely, but she knows how to make a story go on and on and on.

"Anyway," she continued, "it was a beautiful day with blue skies and we all hoped to let our hair down again for Graham's birthday. I mean, what better place to celebrate your 60th than in the park with your family and, of course, with your first grandchild? So, there we are off to the park with baskets of food and all. But silly me was so excited, I forgot to take the picnic blanket. At first, we thought it would be fine as the grass was so soft and green. But, oh dear! Lacy would have none of that. The moment Sarah put her down on the lawn, she screamed. Oh boy! Does that one have a set of lungs on her? It was so bad, other people started to stare. For as long as we held her, she was fine but we didn't dare sit down. No, no, no! When we tried to sit, the grass was too close and the crying started all over again. She just hated it!"

One thing is for sure, most babies don't respond well when they're first introduced to grass. They may curl into balls or pull their little legs up high while intense misery is visible to all. Some little ones have shivers of disgust while others, like Lacy, go into a frantic, emotional meltdown. For many it's a sensory thing and they just don't like the feel of prickly grass on their skin; for others, it's scary because it's new. Remember that until they experience grass for the first time, they've only been used to the sensation of their blankies, tiles, carpets and such, whereas grass can be tickly or prickly. And some poor babies may actually have an allergy to grass.

Because of all that, where possible, it's great to gradually introduce them to grass to ensure a smooth transition from crawling off the blanket and onto the lawn. And another suggestion is to let them get familiar at their own pace.

Yes, going slowly is the key to success but it also helps to pair their first exposure to grass with something they already like. Perhaps their favorite blanket or toy will do as this will provide them with a feeling of familiarity. It's also best to get down on the grass with them instead of maintaining your distance, so be sure to take a spot where it is easy for you to get up and down yourself.

Depending on the size of your backyard, there's a lot you can do with little ones. Pitching a tent and sparking their imagination with a game of make-believe as you move into your make-believe castle is a great activity. The backyard is the perfect place to get your grandkids used to camping and to prepare them for those trips you still want to take at a later stage. It teaches them to adapt to change, especially once they start to spend the night in the tent, and thus, helps with their independence.

If size is a problem, you can always venture out to your neighborhood park or other communal space to fly a kite, kick a ball, play in the sandpit or soar on the swings. It's essential to always remain vigilant when you venture into public parks and never let your grandbaby out of your sight.

Splashing is another amazing idea for hot summer days. You don't need a lot of water, but you do need vigilant focus and attention on the little one all the time. A large bucket of water, a big kitchen bowl or, better still, a little splash pool where they can cool down and have lots of fun, will do wonders. You can add colorful floating toys to make it an even greater learning experience. Tell them about the colors, shapes and sizes of these toys, and just have fun!

Puddle Stomping

After being stuck inside during a rainy day, when and if it stops, even for a little while, a new adventure awaits – puddle stomping. How messy and fun can a muddy puddle be to a tiny tot? Get on those rain boots and perhaps a raincoat (and even if it's cool outside, dress them warmly underneath) and let them stomp around in the puddles. They'll have so much fun (and even more if you don't show them you're worried about getting dirty).

After all that stomping, they'll sleep much better after all the activity and excitement. The actual stomping can be good exercise and improve their muscle strength, balance and coordination. There can be hardly any more of a fun way to enhance their gross motor skills, keep them fit and help them improve their balance too.

Learning *should* be fun as when we enjoy learning, we tend to take up far more information. At this stage of their development with their little brains like sponges soaking up everything, if learning about the outdoors is made to be fun, these sorts of activities will spark their creative neurons and set the foundation for a life of creative expression and out-of-the-box thinking and problem-solving.

Remember, no dirt is ever so bad that it can't be washed away and no clothes so filthy that they won't come clean in the laundry, so don't let 'the dirt' hamper your fun. A little exposure to germs in the mud is not necessarily a bad thing and can boost their immune systems to keep them healthy later on. It doesn't mean, however, that you have to be irresponsible.

Puddle stomping and these sorts of times are also perfect to play make-believe games, have good giggles and just let them explore at their pace. Do be on the lookout for bugs and critters who might also come out after the rain and always seek opportunities to share information and pass on your wisdom while making beautiful memories.

Bug Watching for Beginners

"You must have heard her scream. She was hysterical!" David is quite an outdoorsy person but his wife Lisa is definitely not.

"I prefer the finer things in life," she would always say in defense; and then David would reply that there was nothing finer than nature. This argument had been going on for more than the 30 years we had known them.

Nevertheless, David's always the one outside with the grandkids while Lisa is all too happy being in the kitchen preparing snacks or making something nice for them to eat when they come back home from their adventures.

This particular day was hot and sunny. It was around late afternoon. David went to water their veggie garden with Caleb (then two and a half) following hot on David's heels. Where there are water and kids, the fun quickly erupts, in spite of David trying to keep it under control. So, when he saw a praying mantis on one of the leaves, he quickly decided to draw Caleb's focus away from the hose watering the tomatoes, to the bug.

"They're very interesting," David tried to reinforce his case. "I told him how they catch other insects and we looked at its big jaws, but I also explained that it wouldn't hurt him. As the bug had enough of our attention, it wanted to go, but the lesson wasn't done, so I grabbed it. Caleb was so excited to see me do that, he also wanted to hold it. And he wasn't scared you know! Must take after his gramps. So, I promise, it wasn't my idea, but once he held the mantis, he wanted to show Grandma. And I didn't stop him."

"You probably encouraged him!" Lisa interrupted her husband. "Caleb came into the kitchen all excited. I thought he was holding a flower or a leaf in his little dirty hands. But when he opened them up for me to see, the mantis jumped right onto me!" Lisa exclaimed.

"You gave the poor kid a fright," David teased laughingly.

Oh, the joys of nature! The moment you start looking around your backyard or a bit further around your neighborhood, you'll notice an abundance of new and exciting things to introduce to your grandbaby. It's like a veil is lifted from your eyes and suddenly you start to notice bees (be careful), butterflies, budding blooms, new leaves in spring and falling leaves announcing the coming winter. Everything unfolds before you.

But it isn't just talking to them about what you see that is making for an unforgettable experience, it's also the memories that are shaped around what is seen that makes for lasting, fun-filled moments. It's also about strengthening your bond with your grandkids. As you talk to them and tell them all you know about these bugs and plants, ask them about what they can also see. Count the leaves on a flower or play the *I Spy With My Little Eye* game to guide them to look attentively at their surroundings. The backyard can be an amazing place to expand their vocabulary, improve language and communicate more clearly.

Outdoor engagement can be enjoyed and experienced in so many ways. Not only does it encourage them to think about their surroundings and be more focused, but it also inspires you to be more aware of all the opportunities around you and how to use them creatively to inspire your grandkids.

Pint-Sized Picnics – Enjoying the Outdoors at Their Pace

Picnics can be fun for everyone! However, proper preparation is your key to success and preparation starts with packing all that's necessary to make the day run smoothly. So, pack:

- A picnic blanket

- Wipes

- Sunscreen

- Bug spray

- Water

- Plates and cutlery (preferably reusable non-breakable ones)

- Hats

- Cooler bag

- Ball

- Frisbee

- Soap Bubbles

- And food!

What food should you take? Well, for starters make sure you have enough food of everyone's liking.

Rice rusks, cookies, apple sauce pouches, diced fruit and yogurt are all great ideas to pack at first. But if your grandkids are already toddlers, you can also opt for crackers, cold meats like sausages, cheese slices, juice boxes, fresh veggies and sliced fruit.

As this may be the first such outing, I'd suggest you explore the nearby nature areas close to home. Guide their attention to the plants, flowers, trees and bugs you can see. Show them the different shapes of leaves or explore the different flowers. Talking about what you see and what they see is an amazing way to improve their language and give them confidence in speaking. Make yourself familiar with plants before you go out to make sure you or the little one don't touch anything that may be an irritant or unsafe.

Moving around, running, kicking a ball or flying a kite improves their gross motor skills and balance, and lifts their mood. It's also a wonderful way to ensure they get enough fresh air and will sleep well at night.

Dig into the soil and collect leaves, flowers or seeds of the same size and different sizes. Not only will this contact with nature boost their immune system, but will also be a sensory experience, expanding their world.

What about making a string of flowers? This may seem a task needing quite a bit of patience and while perfection isn't what you're looking for, it'll give your grandkids the chance to practice their fine motor skills.

And when all are tired and ready for a break, lie back and encourage their imagination to go wild as you seek the shapes of animals in the clouds or tell stories about what the worms do underneath the soil!

The Best Places to Have in Your Backyard

Many parents and grandparents are busy for weeks before a baby's birth childproofing their homes. For us, this process was more about improving our backyard. While we put several safety measures in place to keep our grandchildren safe, the fun part and focus were more around transforming our yard into a place where we could spend a lot of time having fun learning experiences with our grandchildren. We wanted to make sure that we could do everything we wanted to do with them right there.

Kid-Proofing Your Backyard

Just like inside your home, there are many places in your backyard where your grandkids can get hurt. So, if you're committed to starting your outdoor adventures with them from an early age onwards, it's best to baby-proof your backyard. I promise that'll put their parents at ease and ensure you have a far more fun and relaxed time.

The following are all things to consider:

- **Dangerous bugs.** As much fun as it is to teach your little ones about all kinds of critters, some bugs can ruin the day. A run-in with wasps and hornets will never have a good ending so it's best to remove any nests in your garden. There are natural ways to do this without too much of an impact on nature so do some specific research or find a sympathetic pest remover. The best remedy, however, is prevention. Also, don't leave leftover food lying around after snack time as that will draw the attention of unwanted insects.

- **Water.** You may not have a pool in your backyard, but a pond can be just as dangerous. Always ensure that your grandkids can't get access to water pools or ponds and that they are monitored at all times.

- **Grass.** Playing on a luscious green lawn is so much fun, but if you don't have green fingers or are living in a dry climate where a lawn is just not a water-wise choice, there's nothing wrong with artificial lawns. But do be picky before you purchase and shop for quality and non-toxic artificial turf.

- **Take care of what's in your garden beddings.** Some plants may have toxic flowers and others bear fruit that can lead to a trip to the ER if consumed. Rather than always being on the watch for what they're doing or worried that they'll sneak something into their mouths, get rid of any plants that could be a threat to your grandkid's well-being. Easy!

- **Chemicals lying around are an absolute 'no-no'!** If you do have any, be sure that they're **locked** away in a garden shed or high up on a shelf. The same is true for garden equipment and tools.

- **Swinging safety.** Do you have a swing in your backyard? These can bring you and your grandkids many hours of fun but be sure they're secure to prevent any injuries.

- **Tripping hazards.** Hosepipes lying around can pose a risk for you and to the grandkids. Many toes have also been cut open against sprinklers peeping out just above the surface. Take a safety sweep across your garden to see what tripping risks threaten you and the grandkids.

- **Touch the dirt, but don't eat it.** Playing in the dirt is a wonderful sensory experience and good for them. However, eating the dirt is an entirely different story. Always be on the lookout for them having a mouthful or two. Some kids just love putting everything into their mouths, even dirt.

- **Think like a kid.** Once you think you're done and your garden is kid-proof, think again. Yes, stand back and look at your backyard from the perspective of a kid. Remember, toddlers can be agile and creative, but the worst thing is that they have no fear. So, see what potential risks your backyard still may have if you look at it from the viewpoint of a three-year-old (even if that means getting down on your hands and knees and having a look from their perspective).

Creating Fun Places

I remember my gran's backyard and the many special places I had like it was yesterday. From climbing the trees or playing in the stream that edged one side, it was wonderful. Such simple settings can become magical places and make beautiful memories.

You can create such fun places in your backyard. Even if you only have a small space available, there are a lot of things you can do. So, pick the age-appropriate options below and get your backyard in tip-top shape to set the foundation for many more outdoor adventures:

- **A place to splash.** Instead of having to carry out all that is needed for some splashing fun, set up a permanent or semi-permanent splash area. This can be a built-in or above-the-ground pool. The best place for this is near a tap and in the shade. Expand on the fun with having a bucket of float toys, squirt guns and plastic cups on hand so that they can pour, dump, dunk and splash to their heart's delight.

- **A place to dig.** A sandbox doesn't have to take up much space and can bring lots of joy to your young grandkids (and sometimes the not-so-young ones too). Here you can keep some toys, plastic spades or shovels, buckets and rakes for them to play. Always cover up the sandbox after play to keep it from becoming the neighborhood's feline litter tray!

- **A place to move and run.** Running is fun when you're so young. Once you remove any trip hazards, you can be sure that playtime will be even more fun. You can also add a few balls of different sizes, as well as kids' toys like strollers, carts and plastic slides. This area will likely take up most of your garden and can therefore be spaced around other play areas.

- **A place to paint.** Painting is messy and therefore best done outside. But it is also fun to paint outside when surrounded by pretty flowers and beautiful colors. A plastic table can easily double up as the art area in your garden. If you have cement paving you can also use this for them to draw on with washable chalk.

- **A place to relax.** Having a strong, sturdy tree can make a wonderful setting for a treehouse once they're a bit older, but for now, it's easier to keep them on the ground. It doesn't require much work to transform an old garden shed into a magical play den.

- **A place to swing.** Swings are fun and help boost children's development on various levels. Be sure that the swing is standing securely and that all attachments are firmly connected. Remove any obstacles they could bump into while swinging. It's also best to place a swing on top of a softer surface to prevent injury should the child fall.

- **A place to garden.** While a very young baby may not be interested in gardening, the toddler may very well be keen on seeing little seeds grow. You don't have to start anything big; a nice-sized pot will do. Get them involved in the process by having their hands in the dirt, planting the seeds, giving water and watching the little plants grow. Something as simple as gardening opens so many opportunities to teach them about nature.

You can start nurturing your grandkid's love for the outdoors right in your backyard, local park or public natural spaces nearby. Make the most of these early days, as that's when you'll start to forge a life-long precious bond with them.

Remember, it isn't always about being active in nature. It can all start by reading them a book outside on a picnic blanket or having family meals on the patio.

Chapter 3
Preschool Explorer Adventures (Ages 3-5)

The simplest toy, one which even the youngest child can operate, is called a grandparent. Sam Levenson

"Sure, she's most welcome to join us. Bye-bye now," Catherine ended the conversation to return her focus to our coffee date. Being the epiphany of elegance and etiquette, she's one of those people who'd normally ignore her phone when in a face-to-face conversation so I was keen to learn why this call was different. As it was, Catherine was even keener to share.

"This is all you, you know," she said with a satisfied smile.

"Me?" I was baffled.

"Yes! Remember how we spoke about taking the grandkids out into nature and how much they can learn in the outdoors?" she asked.

I nodded. Of course, I remembered. After all, it was a topic I'm passionate about.

"Now, when I got home after we chatted, I started thinking. Being a teacher and all, Dennis loved his fishing and camping trips so much...oh well, he just loves to be in nature, it doesn't matter what he does. There's a perfect opportunity for us to spend more time with

Darcy and Oliver (Darcy just turned five and Oliver is a few sleeps away from turning three). Nancy (Catherine's daughter-in-law) didn't take the hook at first, but she came around and agreed that Darcy could go on a trip with us to Lake Istokpoga. Oh, it was such fun. She was so mesmerized by all the color and beauty. Every bug intrigued her and, of course, Dennis knows everything about the plants and trees around that area and was blabbing on *soooo* much, I think he chased most of the fish away," she giggled.

"Anyway," Catherine continued, "Darcy liked it so much as well and got Nancy all excited, who then told Darcy's 'bestie' mom that this kid now also wants to join in on the fun on our next trip. Shame her grandparents are staying in Portland and she hardly ever sees them. So, now that we're off again for a couple of days in two weeks, Darcy's bringing a friend along. It's so exciting!" Catherine beamed with delight.

And I understand why.

Spending time with your grandkids is an amazing privilege. Being able to do it in the outdoors just makes it so much more fun. It simply requires a little awareness and patience (perhaps a bit more than just a little patience) and you'll find an endless number of things to show them, tell them about and keep them mesmerized. The opportunities to pass on information are infinite once you step outside and you'll see how much of a sponge they are to learn new things!

Aren't we lucky to have all these opportunities? But, just as in life, these moments can go completely wasted if you don't notice them. So, let me share the ins and outs of nine of my favorite outdoor activities with my grandkids when they were still toddlers.

The Outdoor Classroom

Teaching Numbers, Colors and Shapes in Nature

Being outdoors is my favorite place to learn and teach, and the enthusiasm I feel surely spills over to my grandkids. Or vice versa, for they too, seem to simply engage with everything I show them.

At this age, kids love to seek things out for themselves and a little competition helps that along and makes the day just so much more exciting. A favorite during autumn is to see who can gather the most leaves as possible.

Then, the exploration starts. This game entails touching the leaves and admiring their hues of gold, brown, copper and red. At times, we'll try to place them in groups of similar leaves based on color, shape or size and then see which of these collections of leaves has the most leaves, bringing counting back to the game.

On lazy summer days, there's nothing more fun than putting a picnic blanket underneath the big oak tree in the backyard and reading stories or lying on our backs staring at the sky. These laid-back sessions can be filled with questions like:

- How many clouds do you see?

- What's the color of the clouds?

- What else is white?

- What color is the sky?

- What color is the sky when it is raining?

Or we can play a little '*I-spy*' (e.g. "I spy with my little eye something pink"). Of course, when it's their time to 'spy', pick some objects that are the incorrect color to test their understanding of what the color looks like. For the most part, this game brings so many lovely memories, but sometimes, other things can be revealed as well. Take my friend Cathy, for example. Cathy realized that her grandson was colorblind when they were playing a game. He'd just turned four and while he caught on quickly identifying numbers, shapes and sizes, he struggled with pinpointing the correct colors. Gradually, she became concerned and urged his parents to take him for color vision deficiency testing. What she suspected turned out to be true. Who would have thought a simple game could have led to that diagnosis?

Some days, it takes a little more patience to keep them engaged but, for the most part, I know we've all had fun with these activities and we persevere. I have always been amazed at how easy learning can become given the right situation and teacher. I could never pinpoint whether it was the abundance of fresh air when outside or just the fact that we were outside with so many stimuli around us, but I've found that being outdoors makes learning more fun and the children are just more open to learning. They just seem to soak up every bit of information. When well-planned (i.e. having enough snacks, drinks and fun ideas on hand), these days can become some of your best memories.

Blowing bubbles can also take on an entirely different dimension in the outdoors. Here they can run a little bit wilder chasing bubbles and you can make it a learning situation by distinguishing between the 'big' ones and the 'teeny-tiny' bubbles. Counting the bubbles and admiring the beautiful colors reflecting off the surface can also be fun.

And if you're ready to take it to the next level, consider starting a veggie patch. Preparing the soil with your grandkids provides opportunities to talk about how the soil feels in their little hands, what color it is or that some things can't be counted, like the grains in the soil. If you're lucky, you may come across an earthworm or two; or perhaps a butterfly passes by and you can explore the colors on its wings. Use your imagination to help stimulate theirs.

Scavenger Hunts and Treasure Trails

We all know how scavenger hunts and treasure trails work and that they can vary based on what you're seeking, where you're looking and how long you want them to last. But did you know the potential benefits this fun activity holds for your grandchild?

- **Improved cognitive skills.** Scavenger hunts are a form of problem-solving. They quickly understand the objective of finding the treasure and then coming up with a plan to accomplish this fun goal. This quest will guide them to explore the environment from a different perspective i.e. not one based on what it looks like but from the perspective of whether it holds a treasure.

- **Sharpen their decision-making skills.** How should they go about looking for clues to lead them to the treasure? What's the best course of action to achieve the desired outcome? What actions will take the least amount of time to find what they're looking for? And if more kids are involved, how can they outsmart the others? It may not always appear at the time as if all of this is going on in the background, but when the hunt is on, it sets the foundation for all of this to take place.

- **It keeps them busy.** A scavenger hunt can quickly turn into a frantic search. It also can become very physical, but being that they're so fixated on finding the treasure, they don't even realize they're busy with a physical activity.

- **Sensory development.** A lot of senses are at play when searching for the treasure. Sight, hearing, smell and physical touch to explore certain surfaces and object are all on high alert, helping them to gather more information that, in turn, increases their sensory information bank.

- **Sparks imagination.** Sometimes, problem-solving is achieved through visualization and, for that, you need to have some level of creativity. When creativity is at work, people come up with innovative approaches to achieving the goal, leading to out-of-the-box thinking and effective strategizing.

- **Practicing teamwork.** When you have several kids playing or they have been divided into teams, they need to work together and see how they can complement each other to outwit the other competitors. This also offers the foundation for good sportsmanship (while this lesson may be a battle for younger kids to learn). Eventually, we all need to learn that there are winners and others who do not win, so this provides an opportunity to plant the seed of how to authentically celebrate the wins of another.

- **A confidence booster of note.** In the hype of excitement and the desire to find the treasure first, there's little to no room to shy away from challenges. There's no time to be scared or timid and, before they realize it, they're exhibiting confidence.

Now, who knew that such a fun activity could have so many benefits?

The Magic of Miniature Worlds - Building Fairy Houses & Gnome Homes

One of the greatest shames of adulthood and growing older is that we often stop playing games. Ironically, the less we play and the more serious we become, the older we get. Also, the less we play, the more our imagination fades and the weaker our problem-solving skills become. It's a vicious cycle. But you can pause it (or even reverse the effect) when you have grandkids.

Imaginative play, like treasure hunts, teaches kids critical thinking skills, but there is much more to it.

It's also an effective way to build their expressive language. Use those moments when building fairy castles or having tea parties with your grandkids to discuss the things you see and imagine. Explore worlds of wonder and magic, and expose them to new words that will build their vocabulary. It's the perfect opportunity for exaggerated conversations to help them gradually build a grasp of the non-verbal elements of communication. For example, "The fairy doesn't just fly away, oh no, she goes *swish, swish* off on her journey to Neverland".

A better understanding of elements of communication like facial expression, non-verbal sounds, body language and gestures, cracks open the world of social interaction and reading social cues more effectively and accurately later in life.

This can be taken further. Social interaction, even if just imaginary, is often part of this type of play and can become the behind-the-scenes lesson of the day. There's hardly any better opportunity to learn how to play nicely and treat others well than when nobody's feelings can get hurt such as when you're sipping tea with imaginary friends. These make-believe moments can be very special.

Such magical moments between building fairy houses and searching for gnomes also provides an opportunity to teach them to manage their emotions more effectively. Even in 'magical' worlds, things don't always go as planned and this creates an opportunity for them to explore different feelings and what's an acceptable way to express them.

Lastly, you can use these moments to guide them into following instructions. For instance, "Gather three white flowers and two green leaves so that we have a gift for the fairy princess," or "We need two short sticks and a piece of bark to defend the city against the mighty dragon."

These moments can be as beneficial to you as to them, so don't hold back. The most important thing, however, is to always have fun, especially if you're visiting Neverland with your favorite little people!

Camping in the Living Room Prepping for Future Campouts

Whether you want to entertain your grandkids on a rainy day or need to prep them for your first outdoor sleepover, building a fort in the living room is as much fun as indoor play can get. Camping in the comfort of your living room combines the excitement of camping with the luxury of indoor life. Instead of the lawn or grassy patches in nature, you can kick back on a carpet.

But you never have to limit the experience just because it's indoors. Of course, the depth to which you're going to explore indoor camping will depend on what you want to achieve, the amount of time you have available and the level of effort you want to put in. Still, there are many ideas to explore.

The simplest tent is probably to move the coffee table aside and put a blanket over the sofa with pillows to add some stability to the makeshift structure. More pillows underneath the blanket offer comfort. Such an indoor tent is the perfect place to read a book or share some stories.

Being in such a confined space also gives the sensory child or those feeling somewhat insecure, a level of certainty, comfort and safety. Sit with them until their emotions settle.

If you have more time or can turn this into an overnight adventure, you can let your imagination run wild and create even more impressive tents in which to overnight. But it doesn't have to stay only with the tent building. You can take the indoor/ outdoor experience a step further by lighting the fireplace and making s'mores! If there's no fireplace to light, the oven works as well to prepare this delicious treat.

During daytime indoor camping, there's plenty of time to play games and have camping fun. Coloring books can turn this into a venture promoting fine motor skills. It's also good to have clean sheets of paper on hand for drawing and creative expression. This can all happen around a picnic blanket with some of the tastiest picnic treats.

And when darkness falls outside, the real fun begins. Then you can grab the flashlights and tell stories of shipwrecks and pirates, or princesses and dragons; whatever tickles your fancy! If that isn't enough to keep their imagination at the ready, you can play the game where you make animal figures with your fingers in the beam of the flashlight.

Backyard Camping – Pitching Tents and Roasting Marshmallows

Once your kids are used to camping in the living room and you (and their parents) feel comfortable taking things outside, it's time to pitch a real tent. Letting them help in the setting up may demand a little more patience from you (and them), but it's an amazing way to get them to follow instructions. If possible, allow them to help with some of the simpler tasks. Not only will it boost their confidence and build their self-esteem, but it'll also improve their motor skills.

The backyard allows you to enjoy the full camping experience of the wild while still being in the safe confinements of your property. Depending on where you are and the season, be sure that you have enough blankets to keep them warm as the cold from sleeping outside may become a problem during the night.

Safety and comfort are essential so be sure to have enough pillows, mattresses and blankets on hand. It can surely be fun to spend the night with your favorite little people this way, but not so much if you wake up with a stiff back or even worse, in the middle of the night with excruciating pain. Take the necessary precautions to make this a fun event for both them and you.

Taking camping to the backyard can be a huge step for them, one that may demand some gentle encouragement. Once undertaken, however, and with the day breaking over your tent, you can be sure their confidence will have grown along with their independence.

Pint-Sized Gardening Planting Seeds of Wonder Together

The biggest mistake you can make when starting a little garden with your grandkids is to go into the venture with too many expectations. Rather, let these go early as then the fun will only multiply.

Gardening is far more than just a fun adventure. It demands some physical work and will help their motor skills develop. It's the perfect opportunity to teach them to follow instructions and probably the most important skill they'll learn is patience. Growing up in a modern society, instant gratification has become the norm for our kids. Considering the many advances in technology, it's perfectly understandable why this is so, but having 'patience as a virtue' will serve them well later in life.

Here are some tips on turning gardening into a fun and learning venture:

- **Decide what you want and what gardening with your grandkids will entail.** Think about how big a piece of plant bedding you want to use. Perhaps a large pot will be better for your situation. It doesn't matter how big you go as you're not creating a showpiece but an opportunity to create memories. After all, it is your garden and it can be whatever you like.

- **Consider what you want to grow.** It isn't just about putting seeds in the soil. You'll have to think about what will grow quickly and easily in your climate; how long it'll be before your garden bears fruit or flowers; if you want to teach them about how you can feed yourself from what you grow in the earth; or show them the beauty one can grow from soil. You may also want to consider adding sensory plants. For instance, the velvety leaves of a Lamb's Ear are lovely to touch. Herbs also awake the olfactory senses and you can familiarize them with the aroma of various herbs. Tasting different fruits or veggies is another way to expand their palate. The garden can also be a place to teach them about being careful with some plants as they may hurt you.

- **This brings me to garden safety.** You don't want to sit with an unhappy child with a thorn in their finger so you should teach them that they can't touch everything. Therefore, always keep garden safety in mind to ensure your garden is toddler-proof

  ○ Don't use harmful chemicals in the garden as you can't be sure that you'll always see when they put something into their mouths

  ○ Consider the safety of your water sources and if it's child friendly

  ○ Keep your eye on sharp gardening tools to prevent injuries

  ○ Teach them that not all plants have equally nice personalities

- **Be prepared to get your hands dirty.** Getting dirty can be so much fun at all ages and, pretty much, there's no right or wrong to it! When they see you get your hands dirty and it's no big issue, they'll easily join in. Let them dig holes and plant seeds. It doesn't matter whether the seeds are planted to perfection. Just keep your fingers crossed that enough little seedlings would sprout into tiny green heads breaking the surface to create a moment of immense excitement.

* **Create something to look forward to.** Let them pick some flowers from the garden to give to Mom or use some of the produce you've grown and prepare a meal they like. For instance, let them indulge in a pizza with tomatoes and basil from the garden. And if you can keep chickens around, draw these into the picture too by getting the children excited about having an omelet or boiled egg for breakfast.

* **Don't lose your cool. Know they won't get it right.** Remember, they're just little kids. Even if you might feel frustrated or tired, still use kindness with your words instead of bashing the optimism right out of them. It may even be that your words weren't harsh at all, but the way they were delivered can bring sadness to the heart of the child lacking the emotional intelligence to process what was said. It's about education and making beautiful memories, and never about confrontation.

* **Know they may lose interest (faster than expected).** A toddler's attention span is short, especially on some days when they're just not engaged. If that day isn't today, it is okay. Try again another day to lure them to the garden to share your wisdom and stories with and help shape the next generation with lots of positive energy.

Puddle Jumping and Mud Pie Making – Embracing Messy Play

Once the rain is over and some sunshine comes out from behind those grey clouds, inviting puddles will be all about and this can be the best time for 'dirty play'. Puddle jumping holds many benefits, like keeping you fit and giving your balance the ultimate workout. But it's also a wonderful way to promote their physical development. Jumping on uneven and, most likely, slippery terrain, improves their gross motor skills, coordination and balance. While it may feel like fun and games, there can still be a lot of physical development taking place.

But it isn't only on the physical side that the magic is happens. No! There's so much more to this. Baking mudpies and serving them to an imaginary family is a great way to spark their creativity and dust off your own. Seasoning can be added with leaves of nearby plants, while little flowers can decorate 'the dish'.

Mud play may be a dirty business, but it's also a sensory indulgence. The texture of the mud, the cool breeze in their hair and being in nature breathing in fresh air after the rain, can flood the senses.

And what makes it more memorable is that mud play is normally off-limits. But now, with Nana and Papa by their side, they can indulge in this forbidden activity of fun and muddy joy!

The 'Outdoor Obstacle Course' for Building Coordination and Confidence

When I say obstacle course, I almost immediately realized that spending time on one of these courses holds a bunch of benefits. But just to be sure, allow me to list only some of the more prominent ways these can and will benefit your grandchild:

- Improved motor skills

- Better coordination

- Advancing their motor planning

- Builds resilience

- Increases confidence

- Expands bilateral coordination

- Sparks creativity

- Encourages teamwork

- Develops their spatial awareness

- Sharpens their focus

- Helps with balance development

So, why do so many kids miss out on this opportunity? Simply, because the most common assumption is that creating an outdoor obstacle course is hard. And it's not!

Here are some practical solutions that make it easy to set up an obstacle course for your grandchild!

Determine the start and finish line. Doing this will give you clarity on what part of the garden you want to use so that you know how much *equipment* you'll need to bring out. Don't forget to keep an eye out for any possible safety hazards. Sprinklers, fences and thorny bushes all fall into the category of safety hazards.

When I say equipment, I don't mean anything fancy. Any number of things on the following list will do:

- Pool noodles

- Hula hoops

- Tent poles

- Ropes

- Play tunnels

- Scrap wood (make sure no old nails)

- Chairs (lawn or camping)

- Flowerpots

- Step stools

- Hockey sticks

- Broom handles

- Sticks

- Play blocks like large Lego

- Plastic toys

I'm guessing that you'll have at least some of these in and around the house.

Okay, so let's get into building the course:

- The start and finish line can be a ribbon on the ground or you can add some drama by resting a pool noodle on two chairs. Or, for even more flair at the finish line, tie some ribbons to a pool noodle bent into a half circle for them to exit the course.

- If you have a play tunnel, that can be the part of the course where they need to belly crawl, but if you don't have one, there's no need to run to the store. You can also use upside-down chairs to create a tunnel or prop hula hoops from the ground to stand upright.

- Plant a row of long sticks of pool noodles to create a slalom through which they can weave. Tie flags to the top end to make it more exciting but placing a couple of smaller flowerpots in a row can work as well.

- Big blocks, small step stools and even a laundry basket can form hurdles for them to jump.

- Two sticks or pool noodles with ribbons tied a few inches apart make for a nice squeeze to slow them down. It's also a challenge that demands coordination and balance.

Remember, you don't want to make it too long or hard. The objective is to have fun, create memories and offer full-round development without them even realizing it.

Outdoor Art Adventures – 5 Outdoor Art Projects to Nurture Creativity in the Fresh Air

By now, I'm sure you can see why I'm such a fan of spending time outdoors with my grandkids. As a final nudge to get you outside with them, I'd love to share the following art projects that are perfect for outdoor play.

Rock Painting

Outside is the safest place to be messy with paint and once those rocks are done, they can be used again in the garden or as display pieces in your home. Let them collect small rocks which gives you the chance to discuss size and texture, color and numbers. Then the creative side can kick in and it's time for planning. Be sure to join in on the fun as kids tend to be more committed when you're playing along and not merely observing them. Acrylic paints are child-friendly, easy to clean off their hands and not too much of a hassle to wash from clothes. I suggest, however, that you still dress them in old clothes for this adventure. Replace expectation with encouragement and urge them to create something of their own.

This exercise builds on resilience, demands creativity, improves fine motor skills and offers opportunities to learn about numbers and colors.

Once the paint is dry, let them find the perfect spot to put their work of art on display.

Chalk Drawing

When I think about chalk drawing from my own childhood, I re-member colorful driveways and vibrant sidewalks, so my advice is to make it big and make it bold. My grandkids always want the biggest and brightest pieces of chalk to give shape to their imagination. Chalk drawing can almost feel like a bit of mischief as it is the only time when drawing on anything but paper is allowed. And it can look so spectacular until the first rains come and wash it all away. This is a double-whammy benefit as it all gets cleaned for the next fun adventure and you don't have to clean up as much yourself.

All you'll need is some larger chalk pieces, sun protection and probably a few softer cushions to sit on. Then, let the fun begin and let it end naturally once the creativity starts to dwindle.

Flower Pressing

Springtime is a time to celebrate new life and make the most of all the pretty flowers in the garden. Take grandkids into this wonderful space to pick a couple of flowers and leaves they like. Utilize this time to discuss the flower's color, the number of petals it has or the feeling of the leaves. It's a very transient activity for once your art project is over, these flowers and leaves aren't good for anything else but the bin.

There are several ways to do flower pressing but the most common and easiest is to place the flowers in a thick book and leave them to dry (tip, put baking paper either side of the flower if you don't want the book to be damaged). With the toddler by your side, however, they may most likely not have the patience for that, as it can take a couple of days or even weeks to dry entirely.

So, when you have a younger audience, it helps to get some paint on hand. Let them cover the flower or leaf in paint and help them press it down on a piece of paper. Once you think there has been sufficient contact and pressure, remove the flower and admire its print. Acrylic paint works well for this too, not only because it is easy to clean, but also because it dries quite quickly.

Splatter Painting

This is just a lot of messy fun, but who knows, sometimes the art created closely resembles an abstract work for which you'll pay big bucks. So, why not frame it?

Have clean pieces of paper on hand and lots more to protect the surface around. The lawn is a great place for splatter painting which is essentially nothing but dipping paint brushes in paint and splatting the paint onto the paper. It's fun and it's a creative exercise so enjoy it!

Bubble Art

This is a simple form of art that can have quite an impressive appeal. In a container, mix about a cup of water with a few drops of dishwashing liquid and a teaspoon of paint (or food coloring). For every color you want to add, you need to mix another container of soap and water. Once all the colors are ready, blow them into the water with a straw to create colorful bubbles.

Now, grab a spoon to let them scoop up the bubbles onto a clean sheet of paper. This 'paint' dries very quickly and several colors can be repeated on the same piece of paper to make the art even more interesting. As always, remember it's about the experience rather than the final product!

I can't even begin to explain how much fun all these activities can be or the number of beautiful memories I have from getting dirty with my grandkids. The best news is that the older your grandkids become, the more activities you can engage them in. So, I'm excited to move on to the next chapter where we'll explore what to do with the slightly older child to keep the fun rolling and be sure they stay engaged in what you have on offer.

Chapter 4

Outdoor Fun for School-Aged Grandchildren (Ages 6-12)

What children need the most are the essentials that grandparents provide in abundance. They give unconditional love, kindness, patience, humor, comfort, lessons in life and, most importantly, cookies. – Rudy Giuliani

I am fortunate. I know it. For me, being fortunate means being healthy and fit enough (sometimes I'm not so sure about the fit part) to spend time with my grandkids. I'm fortunate to live on the coast and a trip to the beach is only a short drive away. I'm equally fortunate to have my grandkids living nearby in a time where family members often stay miles apart and only see each other at Thanksgiving or Christmas. I'm also lucky enough to have many friends who also love spending time in the outdoors with their grandkids, often turning these adventures into a group venture.

And it was during such a group adventure that the next moment played out.

We were about four or five sitting on the beach having the kids play in the shallow water while others were building sandcastles and trying to master the finer art of constructing a solid structure with sand. The older kids were wandering off and seeking shells. It was when Jeremy, the grandchild of a friend who was about eight at that stage, planted himself next to his nana.

"What do you have there Jeremy?" she asked.

"A shell," he said, showing her the treasure in his hand.

"Nan, did you know that shells are homes? Small sea animals live in them and their shells grow with them as they grow. But they die and then the shells wash up on the beach and we pick them up. So, shells can be both pretty and sad."

Jeremy was a deep thinker.

She was visibly touched but I think all of us were also emotionally stirred by young Jeremy's knowledge about seashells and the level of emotional depth he displayed.

"Who told you that, Sweetie," she asked.

"Pops said so the last time we went fishing and were looking for bait," he replied.

I knew Jeremy's granddad was a fun man with a deep-rooted passion for the outdoors, especially the sea, and Jeremy had many times been with him on his fishing trips. During these trips, Jeremy not only generated the most magnificent memories for himself and his grand-dad to hold onto for the rest of their lives, but Jeremy also learned so much about the sea.

To me, this was confirmation of how much more we tend to learn and the more knowledge we consume, when we're exposed to new information while having fun. Learning is just so much more effective when it takes place while making happy memories.

Hiking 101 – Incorporating Lessons Into Treks

Let me start with this advice—if you want to embrace the wilderness with your grandkids, you must pack your patience. Not all adventures are fun and trekking with kids without a healthy supply of patience will surely fall into this category.

When done with proper planning and coupled with the right mindset, you can become the mastermind of a fun experience rich with potential for generating so many rich and beautiful memories. You can also open the door for a wealth of knowledge to enter into their lives. It's when you can share your love and understanding of nature while shaping their perseverance and developing other personal skills.

I gladly share with you the following tips and insights I've learned from my trekking adventures with my grandkids:

- **Let people know where you will be and when.** This can be with a friend, but their parents should also have an itinerary so that they can at least have an idea of where you are.

- **Look at the hike from a different perspective.** The best perspective is to look from the eyes of your grandchild. It's important to take on the perspective of the younger members of your party to be sure you are prepared for every need that may arise on their side. This includes any dietary requirements, general safety measurements and expectations.

- **Patience**. Patience. Patience. Enough said.

- **Slip into your cheerleader role**. The road is going to get long, very long; it may even get too hard for them and it's a pretty good chance that they may start complaining. That's not the time to lose your cool but to become their cheerleader. Encourage them. Distract them. Praise them for how far they've come already. Be the most positive version of yourself possible.

- **Don't expect to immerse yourself in the peace and quiet of the surroundings.** This trip is not for you, it's for them. So, throw any such expectations out the window and know they'll talk at times simply to test the volume of their vocal cords. And yes, they may even cry. But it isn't about what happens, but how you manage every obstacle you come across.

- **Enjoy the journey**. Don't rush to your destination. Firstly, you'll want to make them recognize all the beauty you pass. Secondly, camping spots can be extremely boring to them and it may be even harder to keep them entertained and happy there. Again, use imagination and creativity.

- **Display and discuss trail etiquette.** Being in nature is, after all, the best time to teach them how to treat nature with kindness and respect (as well as with others you might encounter along the trail).

- **Do your research.** Pick an easy and shorter trail, especially if you have a first timer on your crew. Sure, the harder treks may have more impressive nature vistas, but if you have a child battling the chosen 'quest', everyone will struggle and nobody will appreciate what Mother Earth (the wilderness) has to offer. Consider how far they can walk. Are they naturally athletic and active? How difficult is the trail? How far away from civilization are you going? How easy is it to get help when needed? Will there be any interesting landmarks along the way?

- **Hiking is a fun physical activity.** It improves fitness, coordination, strength and endurance. I'd say that's a definite win-win!

- **It's a form of stress relief.** It may not always feel that way, but physical activity and spending time in nature are wonderful antidotes for the stress even young kids experience growing up in an overcrowded and fast-paced environment.

- **Nature unplugs them.** While the likelihood of having internet reception on the track is minimal, the many distractions along the way will also help them forget about their devices.

- **Time in nature fosters a love for the environment**. The more time people spend in nature, the more their admiration and appreciation for the environment grows and, thus, the more they want to be there.

- **There are a billion chances to teach.** Refresh your knowledge about the plants, trees and other natural beauties you may come across along the way. It's also a good time to teach them various camping skills like building and starting a fire or pitching a tent. On the personal skills side, it can help perseverance, respect and appreciation for the simpler things in life.

Make the most of every learning opportunity. As mentioned above, get them to start the fire and pitch the tent under your supervision but let them struggle a bit for they need to become comfortable in the face of challenges and learn perseverance. Allow them to push themselves to build their confidence and grow their self-esteem. Grant them some freedom to encourage independence. Pass on some of the challenges along the way to promote problem-solving skills. Encourage them to give feedback on what they observe to test their understanding, prove their knowledge, expand their vocabulary and grow effective communication skills. It's your job to create a warm and accepting environment where they can feel loved and cherished.

Trust me—following these tips will help you greatly! Yes, I know, some of them may sound like hard work, but the benefits you and they can potentially reap will be worthwhile!

Geocaching – High-Tech Treasure Hunting for the Whole Family

Geocaching is the perfect solution to combine tech and nature and the result can be a fun-filled family experience.

A bit of history first. Geocaching started in 2000 and quickly became popular as it is a global adventure happening in real time. But what is it? Geocaching uses an app linking millions of geocachers across the globe, chasing millions of geocaches that are hidden across 190 countries. To play, you need to register on the geocaching app and from there you'll be guided to treasure hunt geocaches.

Geocaches come in all shapes and sizes and can be hidden anywhere, but they're all linked to the site via GPS. It's the perfect solution to replace the ordinary treasure hunt with something super exciting and, as it is a global venture, it opens your grandkids' eyes to the bigger world.

The idea is to find as many geocaches as you can. When you do, open it up, sign the logbook inside and place it back where you found it. If you remove something from the geocache you must replace it with something of a similar value. Finally, share your fun experience on the site.

Geocaching is an adrenaline-filled venture that quickly gets everyone immersed in the fun of hunting down the geocache. It demands creative thinking and problem-solving, is physically challenging at times and demands patience. It's a sure way to spend time in nature without noticing the hours go by. The fact that it relies on technology to find your treasure makes it easy to stay in touch with others, letting them know you and your grandkids are safe and sound.

I dare you to download the app and log in and see how quickly you get sucked into this adventure (n.b. look in the reference section at the end of this book).

Fishing For Life Skills – Patience, Problem-Solving, Resilience and Tall Tales

I already shared the story of how Jeremy learned so much from his pop on their fishing trips, but there's so much more to such a venture, making fishing a popular choice for taking your grandkids into the outdoors.

One of my favorite aspects of fishing is that it allows plenty of time for meaningful discussions with them. While it's mostly me passing my wisdom to them, it'd be foolish to deny that there've been many times that I was the one learning new things from them! It's also an important time for relationship building. Sitting next to one another on or by the water and waiting for the fish to bite instills a sense of teamwork, being part of something larger than themselves and it encourages authentic happiness when someone else has the big bite. And let's not forget how you can become one with nature and feel the peace and serenity it offers.

Anyone can put a line in the water, but catching something demands some problem-solving skills. You need to think about what the fish are going to do; what bait will be the most effective and how you'll get them to take the hook. Until they do, you need to remain patient, persevere and wait. 'Instant gratification' and 'fishing' are words seldom used in one sentence.

Having them prepare their rods themselves instills a sense of responsibility and taking care of their things, not to mention improving their fine motor skills to get the bait on those hooks without an injury.

Fishing, like life, has social rules that ensure a fun and fulfilling time for all. Hence, taking your grandkids on such an adventure can easily turn into a lesson in life and how to be respectful in all situations.

Use the time you have to instill an appreciation for nature. Discuss the birds and plants surrounding you, what nature does and how to read the weather by looking at the signs. All these chats with your grandkids will set the foundation for a deeper love and understanding of nature and, certainly, many memories will be etched into their minds.

How can you make this a fun adventure?

- Firstly, ensure there are plenty of snacks and drinks to keep them satisfied.

- Pick a fishing spot offering comfort and a reputation for having great bites.

- Consider having at least a decent level of comfort (you'll thank me for that later). A lot of time is spent next to the water and getting up from an uncomfortable seat all stiff or in pain, can minimize your patience and put a damper on the day.

- Take breaks. You don't have to sit staring into the water the entire time. Kick a ball, move your legs, let their penned-up energy escape and return to the water once again.

- Gear up with easy-to-handle equipment and never forget the safety kit. Also, wear the correct clothing, large hats, sunscreen and have bug repellant on hand.

- Think about using more humane 'barbless' hooks and practicing 'catch and release' especially for undersized fish. There are great lessons to pass on when you do this.

The Outdoor Survival Skills Every Kid Should Learn from Their Grandparents

Often, we remember our childhood memories when we practice the skills taught at the time. There's a lot to teach your grandkids about survival in nature, for example, and each lesson holds the potential to expand their knowledge, increase confidence and sense of independence, and etch beautiful, lifetime memories!

Here are just some of the skills to pass on to them. I suggest you spend some time mastering each of these before attempting to pass on the skill as, if you struggle, they'll sense it and you're bound to lose their interest. After all, you want to look good in front of them.

- **Building a fire.** Starting a fire from scratch is a skill that could save their lives one day. Besides this very crucial reason for passing on the skill, it's also exciting to be able to get the flames going from where there was nothing before. It's also a good time to teach fire safety and how to look after your fire so that it keeps going without burning down the entire forest! The latter is surely a lesson in responsibility.

- **Navigation and finding your position.** Today we rely on GPS trackers and other smart features on our devices, but what if they're not on hand? Then we need to fall back to the good 'old-school' techniques of using maps and compasses. Do you know how to use a compass or find your location on a map? Do you perhaps know what signs to look out for in the woods to see where north, south, east and west are? If you're already an outdoorsy person, these things are most likely known to you, but if not, get some training or advice for not only will it help you, but it'll also keep you from passing on incorrect information.

- **Knot tying.** Teaching them about different knots, what they're used for and even more importantly, how to tie them, is a fun way to spend time with your grandkids, improve their fine motor skills, advance their problem-solving abilities and pass on what may be useful and valuable information they can use for the rest of their lives.

- **Building a safe shelter.** This is an essential survival skill to have when you're spending time in nature. Anything can happen once you're out in the wilderness and being equipped with this valuable information will keep them calm and confident in their ability to overcome the challenge at hand. It's also a good way to instill confidence that will help them face many other life challenges, not to mention expanding their creative thinking and problem-solving skills.

- **First aid skills and knowing what plants to use in the wild.** Similarly to the above, equipping them with the knowledge of how to care for themselves or anyone else if anything happens in nature, will provide a confidence boost. Spending time in nature doesn't always mean you have a deep knowledge of the plants available and how to use them effectively, but if you have this insight, share it with your grandkids. Encourage them to scout for the right plants and test their knowledge and understanding before sending them off on their own.

- **Outdoor cooking**. Teaching them how to feed themselves and others even when only limited resources are available, is a wonderful way to empower them. Open-fire cooking demands a sense of responsibility, creative thinking and resourcefulness.

- **Leave nothing behind but your footprints.** Nature is special and we want to keep it that way. So, teach your grandkids to leave no trace behind or signs that they were there. This also means not taking anything from nature that will disturb even the smallest ecosystem. Remember the saying, 'Take nothing but photos, leave nothing but footprints.' While this lesson is essential to preparing the next generation to look after nature, it's also a wonderful opportunity to share how delicate nature can be and how it depends on us to look after it.

Abseiling – Developing Self-Confidence and Trust

Abseiling and rock climbing are brilliant indoor and outdoor activities, and while I don't encourage everyone to do this potentially risky activity, it can be a lot of fun to take your grandkids to these venues or locations, as long as you have the right skills and expertise.

Sure, these activities can be a lot of fun, but there are many benefits that your grandkids can tap into:

- **Improved hand-eye coordination and body awareness.** Climbing and abseiling demand strategic movements. The climber needs to think about every placement of their hands and feet. Their entire body needs to work together to maintain balance, which is amazing for fine motor skill development but also for improving hand-eye coordination and body awareness. Body awareness means they know exactly the position they're in without the need to look. It's about being connected with your body, knowing what it is capable of and optimally utilizing your strength.

- **Better problem-solving and decision-making skills.** Every movement up or down must be well calculated. They constantly need to think about their next move, the best step forward or the safest way to come back down. At times, it can be a slow physical process, but mentally, it can challenge them to exceed their own expectations.

- **Increased confidence and self-esteem**. What happens when you achieve what you believed to be impossible? Your confidence explodes like popcorn in a well-oiled pan. That's what we want for them. They're growing up in a world that will always highlight their shortcomings, so rather give them the boost they need to prepare a strong foundation for adulthood.

- **Sharper focus and longer concentration.** Whether they're going up or down, they must stay firmly focused on the task at hand for as long as it takes. It's how their concentration will improve. And while they're also learning how to stay focused for longer, they'll realize that they're able to do both of these things simultaneously.

- **Better communication skills.** Usually, these venues have instructors guiding participants along the way. The nature of the communication between them up against the rock wall and the instructor at the bottom is essential to keep them from falling. There's no better time to learn to listen well and express yourself effectively than when you're dangling on a rope in mid-air.

- **Being social.** The more you go to the same venues, the likelier it is that they'll meet up with the same kids over and over, and the potential will be there to eventually make friends. It's how their social skills improve and their network expands with other like-minded kids.

Are you ready to take on the rock walls? The sport has become hugely popular and there are many indoor climbing venues around with instructors ready to teach you. Doing it together will be a definite bonus and also give you a better understanding of the technical and physical challenges involved. If it's not for you, that's okay, just be sure you're there to soak up every moment of your grandchild's development.

Canoeing and Kayaking – Paddling Adventures on Still Waters

Spending time on the water can be immense fun. It's a low-investment option and easy to practice, especially when living near water. It's also the perfect place for you to teach them about water safety, paddling, balancing and directional awareness. In terms of other personal skills, it's also a learning opportunity for decision making, staying calm in an emergency and making situational assessments. You may be wondering at this point how you can take them onto the water and still enjoy the time instead of your being in a state of absolute stress.

The following practical safety tips may be handy:

- **Life jackets**. Always make sure everyone is wearing an approved life jacket that fits perfectly so that it doesn't pop off the smaller kids' heads when they land in the water. Make sure it is correctly done up!

- **Prep them for emergencies**. Reassure them and let them know beforehand about what to do if they fall overboard. Sure, if it does happen, it could be a moment of some panic so make sure they have at least some idea of what to do. One way to help this is do some fun drills in the shallows.

- **The right clothes.** Dress them in appropriate clothes to keep them warm or cool depending on the weather and conditions, and that won't be heavy when wet and pull them below the surface.

- **Sun protection**. Hats and sunscreens are essential. Also, remember to apply sunscreen underneath their chins to keep sunburn from the reflection of the water.

- **Teach them safety precautions**. Make sure they know, for example, that standing up without permission is a big no-no as it can cause the entire canoe to go belly up. Again, go over all this when on shore or in the shallows.

- **Watch the weather.** Check the weather and do so for a couple of days in advance. Be aware that the weather can change quite quickly, so stay informed about any possible changes and keep an eye on the sky.

How do you prepare even more for this sort of adventure? Start by getting them excited about the trip ahead. Regardless of what activity you're planning, you always need their buy-in to have at least a chance of making it a success.

Plan your trip and know exactly the nature of the terrain you're taking them into. Prepare them for this too. And if you can find something exciting to distract them along the way, it's even better.

Take your time when you're on the water. Rushing can cause mistakes which can turn into accidents. Rather, take it slowly and enjoy every moment.

Again, have patience; lots of it. Be ready to deal with kids who might get bored after a while.

I'm sure you know the saying that 'practice makes perfect'. While it may not be 'perfect' each time you go out as a beginner, the more you do it, the easier it'll become and the better you'll get at taking your grandkids on this adventure. Never push yourself or them beyond your capabilities. Water is a brilliant place to teach your grandchildren all kinds of things, but never underestimate the powerful force it can be.

Building a Campfire and Storytelling Under the Night Sky

Building and having a campfire is not only good to have as a heat source and for cooking, but it can also allow your grandkids to learn new skills. For a start, it's a chance to teach them an important survival technique and how to take care of themselves and others. It can give them an immense confidence boost. Having a campfire can also be a way to connect and bond with them, especially when you dip your toes into storytelling and heart-to-heart conversations. You'll be surprised by what they'll come up with during those precious times. I often find their perspectives on life intriguing and, while there are sometimes saddening conversations when they open up to share what upsets them in life, these are all important as well. If this happens, this may allow you to step in as a mentor, guiding them with your valuable life experiences.

Time around a campfire is also a good opportunity to pass on campfire cooking skills and strategies. Give them a chance to show their capabilities and guide them to become the cooks they want to be. Being the one who prepared the meal is also a wonderful confidence booster that will last a lifetime.

And once all the cooking and cleaning are finished, you can stoke the fire, kick back and stare into the crackling flames while being surrounded by the serenity of nature. You'll feel your stress fade away and so will they. After a busy day out, sitting around the fire is the perfect way to immerse yourself in well-deserved peace and comfort, and it's just as rewarding for them to calm down after the hectic day.

This is also a time to be more mindful. Encourage them to listen to the night-time sounds and see whether they can accurately identify them. Make the grandkids aware to notice the differences in tone and volume of those sounds. You can hardly get any further away from social media and the constant online buzz than when sitting around the fire. Enjoy the time and set an example of what it looks like to be mindful of the moment and your environment.

This is where storytelling is ideal. The simple act of storytelling opens a treasure chest of benefits. Storytelling is about communicating and being expressive through using words, sounds, body language, tone, facial expressions and gestures. The more you put yourself into the story, using different voices to convey drama and suspense, the more you'll hold their attention and spark their imagination. Through stories, children are introduced to an understanding of a world beyond what they're familiar with in their homes, your home and their playschools. It's where they can learn about different cultures, traditions and rituals. A well-presented story can get them curious, so if you're interrupted with questions, know you've done well in achieving far more than merely providing entertainment. As a further tip, good stories have a start, a middle and an end, and often involve something about overcoming adversity. If you can throw in a morale to the story, well done!

Wildlife Spotting and Identification

"I'll never take my grandkids to Yellowstone ever again!" my cousin Natalie exclaimed.

"You know, we love that place so much, but they're not interested in anything at all! They must take after the other side of the family. They're city people and don't appreciate nature like we do. Such a shame that the kids of today just don't care," she continued her lament.

I wanted to tell her, "No, Natalie, the only shame was that you didn't prepare them well enough. You didn't take them to Yellowstone for them; you went there for yourself, considering only your needs as nature lovers." But did I say that? No, I didn't. Family dynamics can be complex at times and I've learned when to keep my mouth shut. But I should've said something about the manner she and her husband approached introducing their grandkids to the beauty nature has to offer and how that could have been enough to put off an entire generation from connecting with the wild.

The love of nature and animals may run strongly through your veins, but it doesn't mean it's the same for your grandkids, especially if they've grown up in an entirely different world from you. If so, you need to inspire the younger generation so that you can pass on this love. For a start, you need to be excited about your trip to get them intrigued about where you're heading.

Share stories of past adventures and answer all their questions with zest to light their passion for nature. As always, plan such a quest into the wild from their perspective. Think of how to keep them engaged to flex their patience muscle. Whether you're out watching birds or bigger animals, this is a quest demanding perseverance and patience as you wait for nature to reveal her beauties to everyone, young and old.

Once you're there and in the midst of it, while waiting for the biggest marvels to appear, focus on the little things around you. Play games to improve their listening skills by letting them identify different bird calls you can hear. This can become a competition to see who gets the right answer the most, creating a reason for celebration that night around the campfire.

Another competition can be to see who can spot the most different types of animals during your day out. You can take the game to the next level by sharing information about these animals. For example:

- What is hibernation?

- What do black bears feed on while sleeping? (Fat, they lose almost half of their body fat while hibernating)

- Where does the grey fox find protection? (They climb trees and hide in the branches)

Instill in them a sense of responsibility toward nature. Pass on the etiquette and why that should be the norm.

Use these opportunities to teach them mindfulness of the simpler things in life and to appreciate the beauty around them. Just because it is freely available doesn't mean it has no value.

Bike Riding Bonding – From Training Wheels to Mountain Trails

Being able to ride a bike is probably one of the best confidence boosters you can give your grandchild. You don't want them to be the odd one out when everyone else is zipping around so independently on the streets, but you will want them to wear proper gear to keep them safe. Make sure, therefore, that they wear a helmet for the head and pads for their knees and elbows. Also, their bikes should always have reflectors, lights and a bell.

There's no right or wrong time for anyone to become proficient at riding a bike. This is the age when they normally have to let go of their training wheels and take on the road with a greater sense of independence.

- Bike riding improves their balance, strengthens their muscles, increases fitness, burns energy, controls weight and strengthens bones. Guess what? You enjoy the same benefits.

- Like them, you too can enjoy stress release and better mental health resulting from time spent outdoors.

- It increases their focus as they navigate their way. It's fun and results in a surge of endorphins improving their mood.

- Cycling is also a lesson in responsibility. Teaching them how to take care of their bikes and follow the rules of the road are important lessons to learn.

This is probably one of the best stages in your grandchildren's lives to spend time with them in nature. If they're keen on doing things with you and are big enough to take them a little bit further from home, this will allow you to help set the foundation for the next stage of their lives.

A word about trail/mountain biking. You absolutely need to select trails appropriate for their skill level. Some downhill trails are extremely challenging and come with the potential of breaking limbs! Check if designated trails are designed for mountain bikes. Depending on the type of trail, you'll need to assess the risk and benefits. Lightly undulating forest trails might be fine to start with but anything steep should be left to grandparents who are already proficient at mountain biking (see mountain biking with older grandchildren in a later chapter).

Chapter 5
Adrenaline Pumping for Teens (Ages 13+)

"We don't stop playing because we grow old; we grow
old because we stop playing." – George Bernard Shaw

"It's madness! I'm telling you, utter madness. I don't understand why they have to do these things. Can't they have the same level of fun with both feet on the ground?" Gladys' latest venture with her grandkids didn't go well. Perhaps it was because she gave them *carte blanche* to choose what they wanted to do while visiting her. Perhaps it was also because she had no idea what zip lining was when she agreed to not only book the tickets for her grandkids, Simon (16) and Percy (14) but also agreed to do it with them.

"You know, when those two looked at each other with all smiles when I agreed, I should've known something was up. Shame on them for shaming me in that manner!"

It will be a long time before Gladys hands over the reins of their family outdoor adventures to her grandkids again.

Of course, it may get harder to keep up with them as they grow older. They become stronger, fitter and more independent, but that's not how the story goes for us. There are still many opportunities to have fun with your grandkids as they speed toward being young adults. This, of course, should always be fun without injury or needing to face one's fear (like the fear of heights Gladys never knew she had until standing on a platform attached to a zipline high above the ground).

Rock Climbing – Scaling New Heights of Trust and Teamwork

Is rock climbing dangerous? Of course it is! Hanging who knows how far above the ground from a rope is not what we'll ever call a safe option, now is it? But that's not the question I want us to get stuck on. No, I want us to talk about whether rock climbing is a worthy activity to keep your teenage grandchildren busy and whether it leans itself to more than making memories (for memories you'll surely make during these moments of high adrenaline).

Before we get there, let's talk about safety. There are several safety tips to follow that will make such an adventure memorable in many *good* ways:

- **Common sense.** Don't venture onto the rocks if you're all newbies without having someone experienced on the team. Listen to the person with the most experience in the group, especially when they instruct you to do things like checking your partner. This is purely a security protocol during which you check your partner's rope, harness and belay device to be sure they're correctly attached and all are in a good state. Ropes should never be tangled as that can compromise your safety.

- **Don't push yourself or them beyond your abilities.** I'm all for stepping outside of your comfort zone and that should happen on the cliffs too, but it should be a gradual process and not one where you force anyone beyond what they're comfortable.

- **Always be sure that you have a plan in place for any kind of event.** You're in nature and nature can be fickle. The weather report may have stated clear skies, but it doesn't mean you can be assured that it will stay the case. Have a plan B ready. Even consider having a plan C in case plan B fails.

- **Talk to each other.** Also, emphasize beforehand to them how important it is that they listen to you. Effective communication is key to ensuring everyone's safety.

- **Research your route.** The more you know about where you're taking them, the less the chances are of being surprised.

- **Do what's necessary to ensure everyone who went up, came down and without injury.** That means ensuring everyone wears the right safety gear and is aware of their surroundings.

Now, with that out of the way, is it worth it?
Heck yes!

- **Rock climbing boosts their physical fitness** and they won't even realize it. Once they focus on the task at hand and get lost concentrating to make the right moves every time, they'll forget how much strain it is on their muscles, pushing their fitness and building their endurance and muscle strength.

- **Improved mental focus.** Once you're on the cliffs, there's no time to fool around. This is a task demanding focus and clarity. Every move should be carefully considered and you'll be confronted with problem-solving all the way.

- **Facing your fears**. This may be true for you and your grandkids for, at times, it may be daunting to get up and down the cliffs, especially if you're not a pro at climbing or abseiling. It means this adventure could push you and them to step outside your comfort zone, face your fears and walk away feeling victorious.

- **Increased confidence** comes almost as a bonus as it is impossible to not feel confident in your abilities, on and off the cliffs, once you have overcome your fears.

- **Better problem-solving skills.** Whether you're heading up or down, every move is a possible problem you have to overcome. It means their problem-solving skills are getting tried and tested over and over.

- **Practice communication skills.** Climbing is a team effort, meaning effective and clear communication is essential to ensure everyone gets back onto the ground safe and sound. By default, it also means their teamwork skills are being practiced.

- **Emotional regulation improves on the cliffs**. You and they must learn to remain calm while facing challenges, to persevere when tired and to stay patient even when frustrated or struggling.

- **Love for nature.** Lastly, being so close to nature and being able to witness the less trodden surfaces on the face of the Earth is bound to inspire a greater sense of appreciation and love for nature.

Rock climbing is no joke. It's hard work! It can be daunting, exhausting and may require quite a bit of your mental and emotional resources. Once you get down, however, you're bound to feel a deep sense of accomplishment and I'll guarantee, your grandkids will feel the same.

White Water Rafting – Navigating Rapids and Deepening Relationships

What do you need to know about rapids? Rapids come in classes, each one a bit harder and asking a little more from you than the previous. Much like the stages of a relationship deepening over time.

- **Class I rapids** are gentle and smooth-flowing. There isn't much to take note of as the river doesn't have many obstacles to consider. At best, there are only small waves and while this is the best rapid class to consider when you're new to rafting, it also resembles an almost shallow relationship with your grandkids. Sure, you know each other, but there isn't much trust in you from their side and you may not entirely understand their moods or personalities.

- **Class II rapids** get a little wilder. You may have to face small obstacles and maneuver through slightly larger waves. A little more experience is required and you have to trust your teammates, just as the trust between you and your grandkids should grow stronger. The latter is something that only happens when you spend time in each other's company and are there for support when needed.

- **Class III rapids** become moderately challenging. You can expect larger obstacles to overcome and irregular rapids may put your raft in a spin. You have to apply higher levels of skills to maintain your balance and keep your raft afloat. It's surely a much wilder ride, but if you've spent enough time on the water and got to know your teammates and know their strengths and weaknesses, then you can be confident you'll make it. These rapids resemble those many times during the teenage years when your grandkids may face troubling times and feel they can't speak to their parents about their issues for fear they won't understand. This is a time you can step in as their caring mentor, someone with bucket loads of wisdom and love, to help guide them along their way.

- **Class IV rapids** are not for the faint-hearted. They demand advanced maneuvers and exceptional skills. These rapids ensure an exhilarating experience and will keep you on your toes the entire time. While you surely want to have such a deep connection with your grandkids that you can help them through these challenging times, the hope is that you never have to step into such wild waters during their teenage years.

- **Class V rapids** are only for the most experienced river rafters and, unless you are skilled in the water, it's best to steer away from these types of rapids. So, I won't consider them as the ideal 'go-to' activity for the inexperienced grandparent-grandchild duo. But hey, life sometimes has a way of testing us to the point where personal strengths may surface that we otherwise didn't know we had. As strongly as I recommend avoiding these rapids on the water, I encourage you to build a bond with your teenage grandkids that is strong enough that it can survive even the class V rapids in life.

Always be prepared for any level of rapid when going onto the water. Wear the necessary safety gear, ensure proper paddle handling, work on clear and effective communication and, most of all, form a bond with your grandkids founded in mutual trust.

Mountain Biking to Liberate Your Bond and Shape Its Identity

As presented earlier, mountain biking is one of those adventures you can take your grandkids on from early on. But it's only once they reach their teens that it becomes truly an exhilarating adventure (even more so if you've already set a foundation earlier). It's an outdoor activity that brings the freedom of feeling the wind in your hair as adrenalin pumps through your veins and, with this freedom, comes an opportunity to shape your identity and your bond with them. At this stage, it's assumed that the willing grandparent has a higher level of skill and fitness to undertake this exhilarating activity.

- **Boosting overall wellness.** This fast-paced sport is an exciting fitness boost as it will contribute to muscle strength and endurance. The surge of feel-good hormones contributes to reduced stress, anxiety and depression, and will leave you and them in a good mood. Not only excellent for mental wellbeing, it can also improve confidence and self-esteem.

- **Improved focus.** Mountain biking is fast and can be dangerous. It demands focus while testing split-second, decision-making skills. For instance, "Will I go down here or not?"

- **Continuous development of motor skills.** It's about strength, resilience and negotiating your way on mountain paths—all that contributes nicely to sharpen their motor skills.

- **A foundation of health and wellness.** You can use this opportunity to lay the foundation in their lives to be adults who value health, wellness, fitness and living in harmony with an appreciation for nature. The mountains are a place where they can freely shape their identity.

Yes, it's not just about mountain biking! You and your grandkids can gain so much from such an exciting adventure sport.

The 'Wilderness Challenge' for Strengthening Bonds and Building Resilience

There's hardly any better place to teach teens about resilience than the wilderness. No wonder there are programs designed to help troubled teens overcome their challenges by taking them out into the wild. But there's no need to wait until your teenage grandkids are in trouble to take them to the great outdoors. You can use opportunities in the wild to set the necessary foundations to keep them out of trouble when life gets hard (as is guaranteed to happen) by building their resilience.

- **Grow self-awareness.** One of the primary benefits of spending time in the wilderness is that it's free from distractions like the devices that have found a home in the palms of almost young person these days. It's one of the very few places where the persistent presence of social media can be shoved into the background, reducing the pressure it brings. Once your teenage grandchild can shift their focus within, the entire landscape of their personality unfolds in front of them and they can get acquainted with who they really are, identify areas about themselves they want to improve and come to terms with those things they don't like about themselves but don't think they can change. As the grandparent, your responsibility is to provide guidance and support on their inner journey of self-discovery.

- **They enjoy a growing sense of independence and expanding confidence.** The more trips to the wilderness you can facilitate, inspire and accompany, the more you'll notice how they'll start to bloom. Letting them do things for themselves and letting go at times so that they can stumble is important. It's always better to have them stumble in your presence than to have them hide their failures from you. You must be present to help, guide, love and support.

- **A growing sense of respect.** This is a necessity in life! We need respect to flourish, help accomplish our goals and sustain healthy and balanced relationships. Often, it's hardship and the need to persevere, that breed respect. Time in nature is an almost sure way to expose them to these prospects. Through wilderness experiences, you have the opportunity to encourage their respect for nature, others and, most importantly, themselves.

- **Their skillset expands.** There are things nature demands purely for survival that you can't find anywhere else in life. Whether it's pitching a tent, cooking food on an open fire or being able to identify the stars; it doesn't matter. Every practical skill mastered will increase their confidence and be accompanied by many other emotional skills. This is part of the learning process. And the greater their wilderness survival skillset becomes, the more they'll become passionate about other things more than the ordinary interests of modern-day teens.

But why is it such a battle for so many parents, let alone grandparents, to get teens outdoors? To enjoy success in this regard, you need to know what you're up against. Face it, spending time in the outdoors may not be the first choice of activity for the teen who has had little to no experience in the wild.

- The first challenge you're up against is **overbooked schedules.** Today's young people are far more pressed for time than we ever were at that age. Sometimes, they'll overcommit themselves simply because societal expectations are much higher than they used to be. But here I'd like to introduce you (if you didn't already know) to the very important element of FOMO (Fear Of Missing Out). Teenagers, especially, find it difficult to say no to any peer request because of the fear that they may miss out on something important.

- It may also be that they are **just not interested.** We shouldn't neglect the notion that they could be too engaged in other activities and have no desire to spend time outdoors. If this is the case, you'll need to dust off your 'inspirational cloak' and work with your Nana or Papa magic to get them to agree to come along.

- They may be **antisocial!** It's not unusual for teens to spend copious amounts of hours in the privacy of their rooms (or with their devices). They may have no interest in engaging with others (unless it is online) and this is even more so the case when engagement is needed with older adults. Fortunately, you're in control and have the freedom to limit the number of people on the trip to make it easier for your grandchild.

- Lastly, they may be **unmotivated** to try something new or explore fresh horizons. It's so easy to fall into the trap of being stuck to only the familiar in the digital age and having it demand very little extra of you. Just think back to the time when you had to phone up a friend and have an actual conversation or get up and go over for an actual visit. Today, social interaction for our young ones demands nothing more than a few abbreviated words in a language only they understand in a text message.

Multi-Day Backpacking Trips – Planning and Preparation Essentials

Outdoor adventures and wilderness challenges can take on many forms and booking a multi-day backpacking trip with the teens is surely one of them. But how do you plan such an adventure to ensure it is all (at least mostly) smooth sailing?

The following are the steps I found brought me the best results:

- **Plan your trip.** Your entire trip will center around the following two questions:

  - How much time do you have?

  - How far do you want to go?

Your trip should accommodate the time availability of everyone, but also the physical capabilities of all in the group. Knowing how far you want to go (hiking) and how much time you have available (remember it must include travel time there as well), will narrow down your choices of possible trails.

- Another factor to consider when it comes to time is **the size of your travel party.** It reminds me of the African proverb saying, 'If you want to go fast, travel alone, but if you want to go far, travel in a group'. Larger groups tend to be more social, have longer rest stops and travel at a slower pace. Keep these delays in mind when deciding the size of your party and how much time you want to travel each day.

- **How long do you have time to prepare for this trip?** If you're heading out this weekend and it's Friday and you only decided to do so today, then you'll probably have to go for a shorter trip. But if this adventure is in two months, then that's a different story. Then you can plan a much longer adventure.

- **Research the route.** Once you decide on a specific trail, research the life out of it. Don't worry, it'll still be an adventure because nature never lets us down when it comes to surprises. That being said, be sure you know the route.

Other considerations are the distance between base camps, facilities you may or may not have access to, and what you'll need to take along. The latter will also be influenced by who can carry how much weight and how many people there are to carry what you'll need for the adventure. Know what challenges to expect so you can prepare and motivate the younger members of your party in advance.

- **Study the weather.** Don't only consider the weather forecast for the days you'll be out and about, but also look at the usual weather patterns for the area that time of the year. Know what may happen, what to do when it happens and what you'll need if it happens.

- **Consider shuttles.** If you're hiking a circular route, it's easy to use shuttles if they're available. If you're not, you may need transport to get back to your first base camp. Sometimes you can hire these shuttles and sometimes you may find buses run in National Parks, but you may also need to phone a friend to help you with the logistical detail.

- Get to **know all you need to know about the area.** Familiarize yourself with the terrain you can expect to be sure everyone would be able to do and enjoy the hiking adventure. Also, study the animals, birds and bugs you may encounter along the way so that you can share some valuable information about them when you do.

Surfing Safari – Catching Waves and Making Memories at the Beach

Living next to the coastline opens an entire additional range of things you can do with your grandkids, especially if they're teens. One of these fun activities is surfing. Even when you may be more on the 'mature' side, it's one of the most exhilarating and safe (in the sense that there are fewer chances of hurting yourself) options.

It's okay if you and your grandkids are all newbies to surfing. Getting a professional to show you and the kids the ropes can be an experience in itself and having that in common may very well bind you for life. So too with the experiences and challenges of getting on the wave. There's something special about the water and power of the surf that has the ability to connect and deepen our bonds.

However, if you or your grandkids are pros in the water, there are still many other benefits from sharing knowledge, support and strategies to make the most of the waves.

Catching the waves with your teenage grandkids is a sure, fun way to establish a healthy lifestyle. Surfing is not only a great way to increase fitness, but also increase endurance, improve balance and coordination, and maintain a balanced lifestyle.

Surfing safely demands focus and attention. The waves are always moving and if you don't keep your eye on the sea or momentarily lose concentration, you can quickly find yourself in a dangerous situation. So, the more you emphasize to the grandkids the importance of staying aware of the environment and staying within ocean safety guidelines, the better your experience will be.

Large waves can be daunting as well as dangerous. Mastering the giants of the ocean isn't something many of us will achieve. Yet, progressively taking on larger waves isn't only a way of trying new things, but also an opportunity for your grandkids to push themselves (and perhaps you too) beyond their comfort zone.

Surfing is the kind of fun adventure that can quickly turn into a passion. It's also one that can help a family grow stronger. Surfing holidays, for example, can be trips that not only help make great memories, but also provide plenty of opportunities to learn what it means to watch out for and rely on each other.

Surfing can also help improve effective communication, especially while in the water. It can help instill trust and camaraderie between you and your grandkids, and assure them that they can trust you with their lives (and, conversely, that they also have a role to play in looking out for you). From this foundation, trust and respect will grow, turning your connection into a beautiful bond even when on the shore looking out to sea.

Always follow general surfing safety protocol to ensure everyone comes back home safe and sound. These tips include:

- Knowing the rip tides and currents in the specific area you're surfing

- Wearing the necessary gear like an ankle leash so you don't lose your board

- Never going into the water alone

- Picking safe spots to surf, especially if you're new to the sport

- Knowing how well you and your grandkids can swim and never putting yourselves in a position demanding more than what you can do

- Checking the weather and considering any possible changes

that may occur while you're out in the surf

- Taking lessons before entering the water

- Knowing the necessary safety protocols off the top of your head

- Wearing a wet suit when conditions require

- Staying hydrated

Zip Lining – Soaring to New Levels of Exhilaration and Connection

One word to describe my first zipline experience: exhilarating! There's definitely something fun, memorable, uplifting and just plain awesome about pushing your boundaries. Instantly, your body enjoys a feel-good boost as the serotonin and other wonderful hormones surge through your body. And it can also have a longer lasting impact even long after the thrill of the moment has gone.

The beauty of ziplining is that most of the time there are plenty of instructors around guiding you on this adventure. This means that, to a great extent, you can depend on them to stick to the necessary safety protocols and give you a break from being the one in control. However, that doesn't leave you or your grandkids without taking any accountability for your safety.

Safety precautions you can't bypass are:
- Wearing a helmet

- Wearing the right gear (watch out for loose shirts or tops)

- Making sure long hair is well away from the mechanism

- Knowing the rules and what is expected of attendees to a zipline site

- Listening to your instructor and not ignoring the guidelines about the specific course communicated to you.

What can you and your grandkids gain from this adventure?

Well, for a start, it's a wonderful cardio workout. These adventure parks or setups usually require some walking, climbing and then ziplining to another platform where the workout continues as you get down from the platform and travel to the next. It's a wonderful workout in some of nature's most precious treasures and you have the privilege of enjoying not only a thrill, but a bird eye's view of the splendid scenery. Studies determined that it's quite easy to burn as much as 1,500 calories during a day of fun in such a park (*6 Health Benefits of an Adventure Park*, n.d.).

Over recent years, there's been a growing resurgence in the ancient practice of spending time in green spaces. Being outdoors, like when ziplining through or above magical forests, delivers the same benefits; but you also enjoy the added bonus of having an absolute blast. And then there are the other added benefits like reduced stress levels, improved mood, feeling calmer and being more balanced. Ziplining also requires strong core muscles and the ability to hold on (believe me, you want to hold on as tightly as possible when you zip over treetops) and this also increases muscle strength and endurance.

But the most important benefit is that it is a huge amount of fun and is something you can share with your grandkids. In many parks, they also offer a photo service to snap photos of you dangling high in the air. What wonderful memories to share with each other in the years to come. The other advantage is that apart from your entrance fee, there's no special gear and maintenance needed to purchase and you can simply enjoy the day out with your favorite grandkids. Winner!

The 'Digital Detox' Camping Trip – Unplugging to Recharge Relationships

The scene is so familiar in households across the globe: teenagers (and often much younger kids) are superglued to their devices, while communication is restricted to texting abbreviated sentences and expressive emojis.

Over recent years, the amount of time we actually spend talking to each other has steadily been decreasing. Studies reveal more than half of American adults speak for less than 15 minutes on the phone daily while the results for younger generations are surely far less (Shah, 2024). It boils down to us being a generation of people who don't talk much to each other! Considering how much can get lost in translation when we do engage in conversation, the rise in miscommunication when relying only on digital means to express ourselves is exponentially higher.

Far easier than getting these devices from your grandkids is to go where there is no reception or power to keep these devices charged—the wilderness.

Getting your grandkids off their devices is surely one of the most appreciated benefits of taking them camping. But is a digital detox so necessary that you have to undertake regular camping trips even if they're feeling less inclined to go?

I can hear your resounding, "Yes"!

The moment you can get them to disconnect from these devices, the stage is then set for face-to-face communication and thus making it far easier to establish your connection with your grandkids. Camping means you no longer have to compete against a device that they favor over nature. Now you have an opportunity to engage in conversation, grab their attention, impart wisdom and embrace your relationship with them.

Through effective communication you can get to know each other again. It's around campfires that stories are shared, life lessons are dusted off and can be presented, and your grandkids can get to know you as a person beyond just being their Nan or Pops.

Initially, they may be all long-faced and miserable (as detoxing is never a fun experience), but it's during these tough times that you need to persevere for usually it's only a few days in before you start to feel the positive impact. So, don't cut your trip into the wild too short because you'll need your younger travel companions to come around to the idea so that they can see the benefits of putting away their devices, even if only when out with their grandparents.

Mindful in the Mountains – Outdoor Meditation

The mountains have always been a preferred space to reconnect with one's inner existence as it symbolizes spiritual enlightenment. Yet, such a serious approach may not always be part of the plan when you're drafting your itinerary for mindful moments with your grandkids in the mountains.

Still, there are plenty of things you can do to make the most of this higher-altitude adventure.

Be their guide (of course, it is better to have a practice run at home) before stepping into the shoes of being the meditational leader for your grandkids. Here are a few tips for setting yourself up to ensure a successful experience:

- Start by finding a comfortable spot where you can sit undisturbed. If you ever want to know how easy it is for even the smallest distraction to steal your focus and attention, just sit down to meditate.

- Close your eyes and take a few deep breaths to clear the lungs and the head.

- Now, shift your focus to one thing alone. This can be a focal point in front of you or something you want to entertain in your mind. It doesn't matter. What is far more important is that you stay focused and bring your thoughts back every time you wander off.

- Take note of your body and how it feels while you sit in this relaxed position soaking up the serenity of your setting.

- Talk to them and decide on a specific time you want this meditation session to last. Usually, it's better to start with a shorter duration as it may be hard for them to remain focused for too long. But also keep in mind that it may take time for them to get into the entire process, so don't cut your meditation too short either.

- Once the time is up, talk to them. Ask them how it made them feel, what surprised them about these feelings and how they think you can improve on this for your next mountain meditation session.

Meditating in a natural setting is far more relaxing than doing it at home. It's also a way to connect with nature and increase your appreciation for your beautiful surroundings. Meditation can help your grandkids deepen their bond with nature and with you, and it may also be an avenue to distance themselves from their daily worries and concerns typical for a teenager in a modern world.

As you're their companion, guide and motivator on this quest, your bond will improve and grow deeper and stronger.

Solo Challenges – Fostering Self-Reliance in Nature

Solo time in the wild is an enriching experience! It's a time when you come face-to-face with who you are, learn what you're capable of and expand your confidence in your ability to survive even tougher circumstances in life.

Some of the most profound benefits of solo travel include:

- Getting to know yourself much better

- Learning to be self-reliant

- Improving your survival skills

- Increasing your endurance and being able to persevere in tough circumstances.

- Boosting your confidence

- You are chucked right out of your comfort zone.

Solo challenges have the potential to draw the brave heart from even the least confident teenager!

Are your teenage grandkids ready for such an adventure? I want to say, "Of course they are," but only you will know. As a grandparent, it's likely that you're even more in touch and understand the nature of their soul and what they're capable of, than they are about themselves.

So, don't hesitate to encourage such an adventure if you believe the time is right. Remember, a solo challenge doesn't have to be long. Heading out on their own into the wild for as little as an hour can be the first step to enjoying much longer solo ventures.

The following practical tips will make this venture so much easier:

- Let them go to a nearby spot where they can enjoy solidarity in nature without being far away from civilization.

- Pick a spot in nature that is quite close to where you can be, perhaps even close to where you're staying.

- Make sure they have enough supplies to keep them going.

- Check that they have a basic understanding of how to respond in an emergency and have at least a basic first-aid kit with them.

- If this is a longer challenge, be sure to have an itinerary so that you can know where to find them and have a rendezvous location for an emergency.

Trust them. This is not something you'll encourage your grandchild to do unless you know they have at least some experience in the wild, but if the foundation has been laid, let them go so that they can practice using their wings flying solo.

The outdoors has the magic necessary to build, strengthen and restore relationships. It's where you can connect with your grandkids regardless of their age. It's the beauty of spending time in a natural environment and it's never too early or too late to take your grandkids there.

But what if your grandkids have some challenges in respect to their physical or intellectual abilities? Does it mean going out into nature is out of the question? No way! There are many ways to work around the challenges potentially needed to accommodate their needs. Follow me onto the next chapter.

Chapter 6

Adapting Outdoor Adventures for Different Ability Levels

I would love to go back and travel the road not taken, if I knew at the end of it I'd find the same set of grandkids.
Robert Breault

"It only took a little bit of Nana magic," were the words that will always stick with me.

It was my birthday! We all gathered at my home which was, I thought, a rather unusual place for our group of nature-loving friends to assemble. It was Maggie who shared a memory of her Nana—a lady who was equally capable of defending herself against a grizzly bear as she was appreciating the delicate wings of a butterfly fresh out of its cocoon.

"You know, the poor thing," Maggie started, "her parents were always too scared to take her outdoors. It was almost as if she was a delicate porcelain doll that would break the moment she went outside. And she desperately wanted to play with us. I could see her desire to run and kick the ball, but she was never allowed." Maggie's voice changed slightly as she continued, "I still don't know how Nana got her parents to agree to come out with Nana to the farm for the entire Easter weekend but Nana had a way of twisting your arm until you thought it was your idea to start with," Maggie giggled.

Maggie shared the story of how her Nana managed to get Casey, the young girl in a wheelchair, involved in the annual Easter egg hunt. It was a huge 'to-do' every year and her Nana would start painting eggs and making rock candy and saltwater taffy weeks in advance. That morning when the kids all lined up for the event, Casey was still sitting off to the side, but Nana wouldn't have any of that. Nana had made it very clear from the start that it was an 'all-or-nobody' hunt. She'd also decided that particular year, that the kids had to team up and, without Casey, the numbers would be uneven. So, she practically 'begged' the girl to get involved otherwise the day would be ruined. Nana also changed the hunting field to be sure that Casey would be able to get everywhere with her wheelchair and, as she had to have a teammate, it was easy for her to help with the hunt and then get her teammate to get the actual prize.

"But you know the best thing...?" Maggie continued, "All of us played along so well. Every year, it would be a massive push and shove as we all wanted to get the treasures first, but that year, we all played so politely. Without saying a thing, Nana got us to consider Casey the entire time without making her feel left out or bad about her wheelchair. Anything is possible with a bit of Nana magic!"

It's so easy to get set in our ways, thinking that the outdoors is off limits for kids with physical challenges and yet, a small change in perspective can mean an entirely different outlook and mean a world of difference for them. It's amazing how a little bit of Nana (or Pops) magic can be so powerful!

The Sensory Scavenger Hunt for Grandchildren With Autism Spectrum Disorder

A sensory scavenger hunt is a wonderful idea to make children aware of their environment and stimulate their five senses. One of the many benefits a child on the autism spectrum can reap is that it can trigger various sensory responses for them within a safe environment. Through careful and mindful exposure, they can gradually become more comfortable with their sensory triggers and how to respond to them acceptably.

Other benefits revolve around creating an opportunity to communicate how they experience these triggers. This communication can be verbal or non-verbal, and the most important thing is that it can help them to get familiar with their environment and the ways it triggers their senses. So, such a scavenger hunt can also be a way to improve communication skills. Remember, sensory stimulation also supports cognitive development.

One of the easiest sensory scavenger hunts in which you can engage your autistic grandchild is the 5-4-3-2-1 Senses Scavenger Hunt: 5 things to see, 4 to touch, 3 to hear, 2 to smell and 1 to taste.

5-4-3-2-1 Senses Scavenger Hunt

1. Take a couple of deep breaths with your grandchild, taking care not to only tell them what to do, but also to model the action.

2. Next, walk around with them searching for specific objects.

3. Start by looking for five things they can see. Let them point out these things.

4. Now look for four things they can touch and let them touch it. Allow time to let them explain how it feels to them or to show you whether they like or dislike the texture.

5. Look for three things you can hear. Again, point to these things and identify what they are.

6. Search for two things they can smell.

7. Lastly, look for one thing they can taste, after which you can sit down with them and share the treat.

An alternative is to send them to find objects in the garden or home. Give them clear instructions that aren't too complex such as:

- "Bring me something fluffy..."

- "Fetch three smooth objects..."

- "See how many yellow objects you can find..."

Each of these found objects becomes a treasure in its own right.

Other ideas include having a sensory bin filled with beans or rice in which you've hidden certain objects.

For sensory art, you'll need textured fabric, sandpaper, cotton wool, bubble wrap or any other art supplies with a textured surface. Use these supplies to make little pictures. You can also add scented paints and coloring pencils to add another dimension to your art experience.

It's easy to make sensory bottles that can fill in many gaps to encourage their sensory experience. Fill empty bottles with water and food coloring and add glitter or small fidget toys to them.

Wheelchair-Friendly Trails and Adaptive Hiking Equipment

A wheelchair never has to stand in the way between you and getting your grandchild outdoors. Sure, there are some areas where the terrain is simply too rough and not safe for them to go, but there are plenty of wheelchair-friendly hiking trails that you can visit while having a lot of fun (not to mention the helpful equipment and gadgets available to buy or rent making this journey a far easier one).

Practical steps to having a fun wheelchair hiking experience are:

* Do your research. Success is rooted in preparation and you need to explore the specific trail you are keen on taking and what it has to offer. See how challenging the terrain is and whether your grandchild's wheelchair will be able to take on this trail without putting them at risk or damaging the chair.

* Go in a group. At times, you may need an extra hand to help with the chair and it's always better to have some strong arms around that can help with lifting or harder maneuvers.

* Learn all there is to know about hiking equipment for wheelchairs. While there are certain wheelchair brands designed specifically for more challenging terrain typically found on hiking trails, you don't have to go all out to buy them. Having a proper wheelchair backpack may suffice. Other options include an 'under chair' bag, a waterproof cushion and a wheelchair cushion that will offer sufficient support and comfort, providing enough padding when going over rougher terrain.

* Pack all the same things you would normally take on a hike,

but also consider their special needs and anything that your grandchild may require being in a wheelchair.

- Always stay hydrated. Even if your grandchild may not be as physically active as when they would be walking this trail themselves, they're still out in the sun and need to stay hydrated. So, always pack enough water and other drinks to have along the way.

- Finally, you don't have to stick to a formal hiking trail to have the hiking experience. Search your area for horse trails, city parks, ATV trails or even golf courses where you can get outdoors with ease.

5 Confidence-Boosting Outdoor Activities for Grandkids With Anxiety

The more you allow your grandchildren to push themselves, the greater their confidence becomes and the more their anxiety begins to naturally take a back seat in their lives. Parents often must work and don't always have the time to have these moments with their children. This opens the gap for you to step in and play a vital role in your grandchild's anxiety management, forging your bond with them and adding to your legacy.

The following are all activities to consider and, as you'll see, there are many ways to adapt any outdoor activity into a confidence-boosting venture. Consider what activities are age-appropriate for your grandkids and see how you can adapt them.

1. **Walk and talk.** Sitting across from each other and having a conversation can be daunting even for many adults. It can

be so much more for the anxious child. But taking a walk in nature can turn around the entire situation. When there's so much to distract them in their environment and less eye contact needed (e.g. walking single file along a trail), it's easier to keep a conversation going. Sometimes, expressing themselves can cause anxiety to spike, but not so much when they focus on other things. The more they get into the habit of talking, the less anxious they may become.

2. **Climbing.** Never allow them to put themselves at risk of injury, but simply getting on top of a big boulder or something that appears to be a challenge can give them a tremendous sense of accomplishment, encourage them to push themselves a little further when it comes to other challenges and give a boost to their confidence.

3. **Get them to help.** One of the basic human needs is to feel part of something larger than yourself and have a sense of belonging. This is a need present from a very young age, so get them involved, for example, in family chores. Perhaps you have yard work they can help with (make a game of that) or make sure they are included when playing a game with other family members. Consider the anxious child and include them in these group activities to increase their sense of belonging and help them feel they are contributing.

4. **Be an example of confidence.** Children tend to learn far more from observing us than from us 'telling' them what to do. So, always be an example of confidence when you spend time with them outdoors. Take care to use positive language and body language supporting your words. They watch you

so make sure it's a worthy show to observe.

5. **Praise them.** Do you ever think about the fact that for
most of our lives, the world is telling us that we're not good
enough, smart enough or pretty enough? And that is sadly
not even where the list of 'not enough' ends. Therefore, as
long as you have them under your roof or in your company,
use the time to tell them they are 'enough'. Give authentic,
meaningful and directed praise, and see how your anxious
grandchild starts to bloom in your presence.

What are your favorite outdoor activities with your anxious grandchild? Consider how you can turn these moments into confidence-boosting ventures.

The Outdoor Quiet Space for Introverted or Highly Sensitive Grandchildren

There's so much happening outdoors that most kids reap pure joy
from being in the fresh air. It's easy to keep kids, especially the younger
ones, engaged all the time. But that's not the case for all kids. For
instance, shy or introverted kids may have a hard time relaxing and
playing freely in a public park. They may find it hard to relax and,
while you want them to enjoy themselves, the complete opposite may
be the case and you end up with a stressed and miserable child.

The 'outdoors' is where there are often loud sounds, bright lights
or strangers. These can all translate as threats to your introverted or
highly sensitive grandchild. But there's plenty you can do to transform
the outdoors into a place they too can enjoy. With a little creative
thinking, a lot becomes possible.

Why not make a start by transforming your backyard? Typically, a backyard is a relatively secluded space, but there may still be a noisy neighbor or even their dog that keeps on barking through the fence. The latter is surely something you'll have to address diplomatically with your neighbor, but there's more you can do:

- Curtains, walls, dividers or living walls filled with plants can do a lot to reduce the noise and give you some privacy while spending time outside with your sensitive grandchild. Consider the fence you have around your backyard to see if it offers sufficient privacy.

- Fishponds and water features are usually very serene and you may consider installing (if your backyard allows for it) a fishpond or water feature in a quieter corner of your backyard.

- Does your backyard have a tree that can hold a treehouse? A well-built treehouse can offer privacy and be a perfect hiding place when the world is getting too much. If you invest sufficient time and effort into the structure, it can become a secret safe space from where you both can watch the garden birds and even spy on the neighborhood. How much fun will that be?

- Remove any objects that can startle them. For instance, some kids may be scared of large garden gnomes or reflective objects dangling from trees to keep birds away, while a neighbor peeping unexpectedly over your wall can also give them a fright. Remember, every time your grandchild feels uncomfortable in your backyard or any other outdoor space, it'll become harder to get them to return to that space. So, defend the privacy and serenity of this space as much as you can.

But what about venturing further out than the backyard? Jenny, a good friend of mine, faced this challenge. Her four-year-old grandson, Joshua, struggled to be around strangers. But Jenny had a super plan and made him a cloak. She convinced Joshua (and got the family to play along) that once he wore his cape, he would be invisible to strangers. He believed they could look at him but wouldn't see him. This played wonderfully with his interest in cape-wearing superheroes and ensured he could go to the park. Slowly, it gave Joshua more and more confidence to be among strangers until he was ready to let go of his magical cape altogether!

Older kids may not want to be this silly and, of course, will not fall for the idea of a magical cape, but you can help them shut out the world in other ways. Soundproof headphones, for example, are just one way to reduce sensory overload, making them feel more at ease outside.

Modifying Classic Outdoor Games for Grandkids With Mobility Challenges

I've always found it immensely relaxing to sit in my backyard and watch my grandkids play tag, kickball or any other fun activity that would just have them run around bursting out in laughter. But that isn't a privilege all grandparents have—some may face the challenge of having a grandchild with challenges of mobility, visual impairment, deafness or intellect.

The good news is that your hands aren't tied and, here too, there are steps you can take to accommodate their special needs:

- **Basketball**, or simply tossing a ball, is something that kids can do even while sitting down, making it a good option for grandparents whose grandkids may struggle with mobility.

There are many different variations of this game too. While simply tossing the ball will be fine, it can be more fun to make it more of a game and score. Starting at 20, play it with music and the one who has the ball in their hands when the music stops loses a point. The game can last quite a while and you can prepare longer and shorter pieces of music.

- Depending on the layout and size of your backyard, this can easily be the perfect setting for **playing hide and seek**. It may mean that you allow more time for the child with mobility concerns to find a good hiding spot or you may have to work in teams. Nana and your grandchild hide, for example, and Pops needs to find them.

- There are also plenty of games involving **bubbles.** They can catch the bubbles, count the bubbles or even blow them for you to pop.

- Is there an orchard nearby? Take them **fruit picking**. Orchards are usually maintained in a manner that even wheelchairs have access and while your grandchild may not always be able to get up to pick the fruit, it's a fun adventure reminiscent of a treasure hunt to find the ripest fruit.

- **Gardening** is another outdoor activity that can be easily adjusted to accommodate the needs of your grandchild. For instance, if they can't get down to work the bedding with their hands, you can also plant in pots on a table and have them work the soil on a table at a comfortable height. This will make it easier for them to get involved in the process and have fun digging with their fingers in the soil.

- Working on higher surfaces makes it much easier for everyone as even your back can get a break from bending and
  getting up and down. **Rock painting** is another activity you
  can take outdoors. Allow their creative energy to flow and see
  what other things you can do with natural material found
  outdoors.

There are lots of things you can do. In the end, it all depends on
the age of your grandchild, what they're capable of doing and how
physically fit you are to accommodate some of these games.

6 Calming Outdoor Activities to Help Grandchildren Cope with ADHD

Kids with ADHD are so often misunderstood and overly judged, it's
even more essential that they find acceptance, love and freedom to be
themselves in your company. Due to their high level of energy and
the constant need to move around, the outdoors is a fantastic place
to keep them entertained, forge your bond with them and give them
the freedom to be themselves without being too concerned about any
possible disturbance they might make and creating a situation where
they may be unfairly judged.

How can you keep them entertained?

Get Moving

The more they can be active and run freely, the happier the ADHD
child will be; and there is no better place for them to run around than
in the outdoors. So, taking them hiking is a perfect way to get rid of
their excess energy and, once you've taken care of that, you can engage

them on a different level. For instance, longer conversations can flow as you walk, opening an opportunity to pass on meaningful 'words of wisdom', make an impact on their mental and emotional state or simply teach them about the beauty of nature.

Another option is to go rock climbing.

While you'll be making magnificent memories, this is also a time to improve your focus, balance, perseverance and coordination. On their mental and emotional levels, you'll start to witness a longer concentration span, greater confidence and growing self-esteem.

Get Creative

Spending time outdoors tends to spark a greater sense of creativity. Here your ADHD grandchild can immerse themselves in their imagination, fight off imaginary dragons and build forts. Having a treehouse at your disposal is, of course, another effective way to attract and keep their interest.

Except for imaginary games, you can also encourage them to actually create or build something. Rock painting, rock art and even building a small rock garden, can keep them fully engaged, increase their attention span and even contribute to a sense of greater responsibility.

Making objects from clay to showcase in the garden is another way to add value to their creations and give them a sense of accomplishment. Ultimately, it doesn't matter what type of creative medium you choose, just immerse yourself and them in the freedom the outdoors offers.

Have a Picnic

A picnic is always a good backup plan for when the outdoors calls you and you've run out of ideas. Whether you want to go outside by making a campfire and get your grandkids involved in open fire cooking, making s'mores, barbequing sausages on a stick or having a more refined picnic on a blanket with a basket full of healthy but tasty snacks, doesn't really matter. Use the open space to play frisbee or kickball. Or how about bringing along a kite and not only can you explain the dynamics of why a kite is flying, but you can also introduce them to the freedom of flight.

Star Gazing

There is no reason why you can't get out at night. The beauty of stargazing is that you can do it right in your backyard (while being further away from the city lights will ensure you see more stars). Star gazing is a wonderful way to calm them down and bring elevated energy levels to rest after a busy day. This may mean you are teaching them about the constellations or simply trying to see who can see the most shooting stars.

You'll even be surprised how many meaningful conversations the stars can spark. I remember one beautiful summer evening when I was lying on my back on the lawn surrounded by my grandkids and their friends (two of whom had been diagnosed with ADHD). These two boys were initially quite a handful to manage in the dark, but eventually, they got the message that all of us just wanted to lie down and look at the stars. As time went by, a competition developed to see who could count the most shooting stars. From there, I had to explain about wishing on a star and, as the night continued, I was peppered with questions like:

• Why do stars shine?

- How many stars are there?

- What's a shooting star?

- Who shoots the star?

- Does it hurt the star when it flies through the sky?

- Why can't we see the stars during the daytime?

It was a wild night and I was exhausted afterward as they kept me on my toes with a million and one questions. It remains, however, as one of my best memories, having all these kids, including the ones whose parents thought they were never going to settle down, hanging on my every word.

Play Games to Keep Them Focused

The outdoors, whether in your backyard, a public open space or the wilderness, offers a perfect foundation for higher levels of activity, while at the same time engaging them mentally, improving their focus and concentration, and boosting their confidence.

ADHD kids may be considered to be difficult to handle, but this may mostly be due to a lack of understanding by those in society who may have little to no understanding of how such children are and the challenges that a family managing children with ADHD have to deal with.

Some of the activities that work well outside are:

- Musical games, like musical chairs

- Dancing like trees

- Rope jumping

- Hula hooping

- Balloon volleyball

There is, however, one game that's brilliant to keep them focused. This game is such an oldie that you may even be surprised to read about it here. I am talking about 'Follow the Leader'.

'Follow the Leader' is a fun way to keep them engaged, notice what others are doing and copy the same moves exactly as the leader or they're out. Have you ever thought about how much attention and focus 'Follow the Leader' teaches in a fun way without them even realizing that they're busy lengthening their attention span?

Visit a Petting Zoo

A petting zoo is another fun outdoor space I haven't mentioned yet. Here you can bring your grandkids up close and personal to animals, fostering a deeper understanding and appreciation about each type of animal, but also let the grandkids' kindness a chance to surface. They can feed the animals, learn all about nurturing and show affection while gaining a greater appreciation for nature.

Petting zoos can be exciting and provide so many opportunities for learning as well as lots of moments of laughter.

The outdoors has something to offer everyone and, with a little creativity, it's really a case of 'no child needing to stay behind'!

Chapter 7
At The End Of The Day...

Grandchildren are a grandparent's link to the future. Grandparents are the child's link to the past." – Unknown

There are many achievements in my life of which I am immensely proud. These things are my legacy. But the one thing that has always been my greatest accomplishment, the one thing that is still continuously expanding my legacy and adding value to my life, is the relationship I have with my grandkids.

Your legacy will be the lasting memory of you! It'll be the imprint you leave on the world, a testimony that you were here, but also, the difference you made in the lives of those near and dear to you. Sometimes, even with the lives of those whom you hardly knew.

The part of my legacy I want to share with my grandkids centers around nature, the love of the outdoors and the freedom I feel when I immerse myself in the wilderness. And I know that I don't have to wait until I've gone from this world to know that I've been successful. I've already been able to see that my legacy has started to shape their lives.

And here is my final story for this book.

It was a dreamy Saturday morning. While it was still early, it was obvious that the day was going to a hot one. There was already a haziness hanging over the lake and, except for the birds happily chirping in the nearby trees and the buzzing of bugs in the rough patches bordering the water, there was not a sound. I must have been around five years old, but I felt like an adult.

Inside my chest, my heart was exploding with excitement. Gramps took me on his 'fishing boat' and we were sitting in the middle of the lake. When I say, 'fishing boat', my memory of it back then was that it felt so big and exciting that it might as well have been a luxurious cruiser. But I realize now, it was possibly no more than a small rowing boat without a motor. I remember we went way out to the middle and deepest part of the lake, a part where I'd never been allowed. It was both scary and exhilarating.

Over the years, I've processed that special moment. Often, as my emotional intelligence and understanding of life grew, I realized more and more things that happened that day. My existence felt validated, I felt seen, important, accepted, special, and, most of all, loved.

I'm sharing this memory with you for a reason. There wasn't much conversation that took place on the water that day (Gramps told me it would scare the fish away), but it remains one of the most meaningful memories of my childhood. Simply being invited to spend such a time with my gramps meant so much. As the years went by, there were other moments when we engaged in deep and meaningful conversations, and many pearls of wisdom were passed to me, but that specific memory of the day on the lake remains special.

What I'm saying is that, throughout the book, I've shared practical steps, ideas, strategies and helpful tips to help you get your grandkids outside in the hope you'll have a meaningful impact on their lives and wonderful memories will be created. Sometimes, however, our plans just don't work out as we've hoped, someone may not be in the best of moods and it may seem as if all your good intentions fail. If and when that happens, remember that you're still giving them your time and time is the most precious gift you can offer to anyone. Spending time with your grandkids is the foundation from which all other good things sprout.

So, my best advice is to make time, spend time, invest time and enjoy the time you have with your grandkids.

And speaking of time, I hope you've enjoyed the time reading this book and you've enjoyed it as much as I have writing. I'd also like to ask that you take a little of your time to leave a review so that more grandparents like you can get guidance on what to do with the time we have with our grandkids and how, they too, can make a lasting impact on their grandkids lives.

Thank you and 'happy trails'.

Ruby

References

Adrenaline quotes. (n.d.). Brainy Quote. https://www.brainyquo te.com/topics/adrenaline-quotes

Almekinder, E. (2020, January 24). *The N.E.A.T. way to exercise for a longer, healthier life.* Blue Zones. https://www.bluezones.com/20 20/01/the-neat-way-to-exercise-for-a-longer-healthier-life/

Andrea. (2019, April 27). *The ultimate guide to hiking with kids: Kid-friendly hiking trails, tips, and gear.*

Embracing the Wind. https://embracingthewind.com/guide-to -hiking-with-kids/

Benefits of muddy puddle play for children. (2023, November 7). Best Preschool
https://bestpreschool.ro/2023/11/07/benefits-of-muddy-puddle-pl ay-for-children/#:~:text=Muddy%20puddle%20play%20is%20more

Cherry, K. (2024, August 8). *9 Fun activities for kids with ADHD.* Very well Mind. https://www.verywellmind.com/fun-activities-for -kids-with-adhd-5235327#toc-go-stargazing

Crider, C. (2021, September 20). *When can newborns go outside?* Healthline.
https://www.healthline.com/health/baby/when-can-newborns-go-o utside#expert-opinion

Dee. (2024, May 15). *13 White water rafting tips for beginners.* Southeastern Expeditions. https://southeasternexpeditions.com/13 -white-water-rafting-tips-beginners/

Fabian-Weber, N. (2023, October 6). *Why do babies avoid grass? Experts explain the bizarre but adorable instinct.* Care.com

http://www.care.com/c/why-do-babies-avoid-grass

Fanelli, L. (n.d.). *The benefits of bird watching for kids.* Toms of Maine. https://www.tomsofmaine.com/good-matters/thinking-sus tainably/the-benefits-of-bird-watching-for-kids

First aid kit for the outdoors. (n.d.). Will4Adventure. https://will 4adventure.com/advice/first-aid-kit-for-the-outdoors/

First-aid checklist. (n.d.). REI Expert Advice. https://www.rei.co m/learn/expert-advice/first-aid-checklist.html

5 Great outdoor activities for children with ADHD. (n.d.). Brain Balance Centers. https://www.brainbalancecenters.com/blog/great -outdoor-activities-for-children-with-adhd

5 Reasons why you should surf with your teens. (2018, June 27). Kalon Surf. https://kalonsurf.com/blog/5-reasons-why-you-should -surf-with-your-teens/

Funny grandparent quotes. (2024). A-Z Quotes. https://www.azq uotes.com/quotes/topics/funny-grandparent.html?p=2

G, B. (2023, May 8). *8 Benefits of rock climbing for kids.* Brooklyn Boulders.

https://brooklynboulders.com/blogs/news/8-benefits-of-rock-climb ing-for-kids

Gifford, E. (n.d.). *10 Indoor camping ideas your kids will love.* HGTV.

https://www.hgtv.com/lifestyle/family/kids-and-babies/indoor-c amping-ideas-for-kids-pictures

Go, C. (2023, September 4). *First aid for outdoor adventures: Essential preparation for hiking, camping, and traveling.* First Response Safety Training. https://www.firstresponsecpr.com/blog/outdoor-first-aid/

Holecko, C. (2022). *5 Backyard play ideas for babies.* Highlights. https://parents.highlights.com/5-backyard-play-ideas-babies

How do sensory activities help autism? (2024, January 24). Seashell. https://www.seashelltrust.org.uk/how-do-sensory-activities-help-autism/

How to make a backyard obstacle course for kids. (n.d.) Hands-on as We Grow. https://handsonaswegrow.com/obstacle-course-kids-fort-magic/

How to plan a backpacking trip. (n.d.). Rei Co-Op. https://www.rei.com/learn/expert-advice/backpack-planning.html?srsltid=AfmBOooJxaNRqoHuhX-9ndamHGE39rRvDdYA_HBqkoTP6HqyytoEibsY

Introducing your baby to the outdoors - 7 Safety tips. (2020). Playground Professionals. https://playgroundprofessionals.com/playground/nature/introducing-your-baby-outdoors-7-safety-tips

Lifelong outdoor skills every kid should be taught. (2023, December). Great Rivers Council. https://grcbsa.org/2023/12/01/outdoor-skills/

Malkin, N. (2022, March 25). *13 Ways to childproof your yard and garden.* Bob Vila. https://www.bobvila.com/articles/childproof-yard-and-garden/

Millar, J. (2024). *Top 10 reasons to consider rock climbing for your teenager this summer.* Stone Mountain Adventures. https://www.sma-summers.com/juds-blog/the-top-10-benefits-of-outdoor-rock-climbing-for-teenagers

Moeller, S. (2024, April 3). *10 Ways to get grandkids into gardening.* AARP.
https://www.aarp.org/home-family/your-home/info-2024/gardenin g-with-grandkids.html

9 reasons why kids should spend time in nature. (2023, May 2). Gulo in Nature.
https://guloinnature.com/9-reasons-why-kids-should-spend-time-in -nature/

Paul, D. (2024, May 2). *9 Unexpected benefits of scavenger hunts for kids.* That's so Montessori.
https://thatssomontessori.com/benefits-of-scavenger-hunts/

Rahman, C. (2017, January 7). *5 Tips for wheelchair hiking.* United Spinal Association.
https://unitedspinal.org/5-tips-wheelchair-hiking/

Randall, B. (2019, September 19). *Beginner tips for canoeing with kids.* Run Wild My Child.
https://runwildmychild.com/canoeing-with-kids/

Reynolds, G. (2022, February 2). What the "Active Grandparent Hypothesis" can tell us about aging well. *The New York Times.*
https://www.nytimes.com/2022/02/02/well/move/aging-exercise-gr andparents.html

Reynolds, G., Conrad, C., & TerBush, C. (2024, January 1). *Are you fit for your age? Try our fitness tuneup to find out.* The Washington Post.
https://www.washingtonpost.com/wellness/interactive/2024/fitness -test-by-age-exercise/

Shah, K. (2024, July). *How long do Americans talk on calls in a day?* You go.
https://business.yougov.com/content/49894-how-long-do-american s-talk-on-calls-in-day

7 Ways babies benefit from getting outside. (2024). Happiest Baby.
https://www.happiestbaby.com/blogs/baby/nature-benefits-baby

6 Health benefits of an adventure park. (n.d.). The Adventure
Park.
https://myadventurepark.com/health-benefits-of-an-adventure-park

6 Key reasons to spend more time outdoors with your baby. (2021,
June 3). Schoolhouse Day Care.
https://schoolhouse-daycare.co.uk/blog/6-reasons-to-take-your-bab
y-outside/

Spivey, M. (2022, October 30). *What is imaginative play and why
is it important for young children?* Start Early.
https://www.startearly.org/post/imaginative-play/#:~:text=Through
%20imaginative%20play%20children%20learn

Ultimate list of outdoor gear for kids. (2022, August 22). Run Wild
My Child.
https://runwildmychild.com/outdoor-gear-for-kids/

Ward, M. (2019, May 21). *Baby's first picnic in the park.* To & Fro.
http://www.toandfroblog.com/2019/05/baby-friendly-picnic-tips.h
tml

What is geocaching? (2018, March 5). Geocaching.
https://www.geocaching.com/blog/2018/03/what-is-geocaching/

Wilder, J. (2022, August 18). *Does adventure therapy work? 5 Benefits of wilderness therapy for troubled teens.* All Kinds of Therapy.
https://www.allkindsoftherapy.com/does-adventure-therapy-work-5
-benefits-of-wilderness-therapy-for-troubled-teens

Made in the USA
Columbia, SC
05 February 2025

53350464R00083